Inclusive Education
International Policy & Practice

Ann Cheryl Armstrong,
Derrick Armstrong & Ilektra Spandagou

Los Angeles | London | New Delhi
Singapore | Washington DC

SAGE Publications Ltd
1 Oliver's Yard
55 City Road
London EC1Y 1SP

SAGE Publications Inc.
2455 Teller Road
Thousand Oaks, California 91320

SAGE Publications India Pvt Ltd
B 1/I 1 Mohan Cooperative Industrial Area
Mathura Road
New Delhi 110 044

SAGE Publications Asia-Pacific Pte Ltd
33 Pekin Street #02-01
Far East Square
Singapore 048763

Library of Congress Control Number 2009929119

British Library Cataloguing in Publication data

A catalogue record for this book is available from the British Library

ISBN 978-1-84787-940-0
ISBN 978-1-84787-941-7 (pbk)

Typeset by C&M Digitals (P) Ltd, Chennai, India
Printed in TJ International, Padstow, Cornwall
Printed on paper from sustainable resources

Mixed Sources
Product group from well-managed
forests and other controlled sources
www.fsc.org Cert no. SGS-COC-2482
© 1996 Forest Stewardship Council
FSC

Books are to be returned on or before
the last date below.

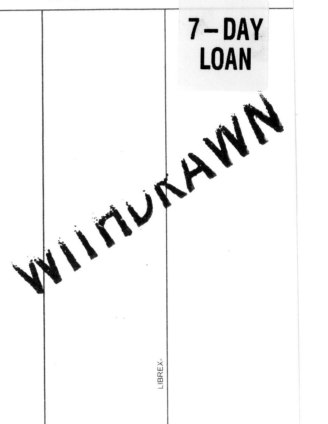

LIBREX-

Contents

About the Authors

Dr Ann Cheryl Armstrong is Director, Division of Professional Learning in the Faculty of Education and Social Work at the University of Sydney. Ann Cheryl has worked in inclusive education and professional development at an international level for 23 years and has extensive experience as a teacher, teacher educator, research manager, project manager and programme leader. She has worked in countries throughout the Caribbean, the UK, Australia and Asia. Before emigrating to Sydney in February 2005, she was employed with the University of Sheffield, UK, in the School of Education as Director of the Caribbean Distance Education Programme. Ann Cheryl has held senior positions in two national World Bank projects and has acquired extensive experience in networking with government and non-government agencies for the provision of educational and social services and training. She has presented at numerous national and international conferences and contributed on various committees and panels. At present she is on the University of Sydney Indigenous Education Advisory Committee as well as on the Sydney Region (Schools) Planning Group for Aboriginal Education and Training.

Professor Derrick Armstrong was appointed Deputy Vice-Chancellor (Education) and Registrar in December 2008. His responsibilities at the University of Sydney include all aspects of the Student Experience: Learning and Teaching, Student Administration and Support, Indigenous Education, Student Recruitment and Social Inclusion. Prior to this he was Dean of the Faculty of Education and Social Work at the University of Sydney. His research has focused on issues of social inclusion and exclusion in education and the ways in which disadvantage and 'deviance' are identified and managed by professionals, social agencies and institutions working with children and young people. Derrick is author, co-author and editor of eight books and more than a hundred journal articles, book chapters and international conference papers.

Dr Ilektra Spandagou is a lecturer in inclusive education in the Faculty of Education and Social Work at the University of Sydney. She worked as a special teacher in inclusive settings before completing her PhD at the University of Sheffield, UK. She has been involved in pre-service and post-graduate teacher education and teacher training, retraining and specialization programmes in the area of inclusive and special education in Greece and Australia. Her research interests include inclusive education, disability studies and classroom diversity and pedagogy. Her work currently focuses on teacher education for inclusion and the role of teachers' attitudes.

Preface

Inclusive education has become fashionable. Like all fashions its origins lie in the haute couture imagination, and from there has spread out, first into mass production for the high street and, thereafter, rapidly into the world of cheap replicas and reproductions. The world of high fashion is a strange world of creativity and abstraction, a world of extreme self-confidence and banal triviality. Unwearable and unaffordable for most people, it nonetheless, through translation and adaptation, finds its way into wardrobes across the world, often without us knowing anything about the history of the garments we have bought: neither the fashion houses that have created them nor the sweatshops that produced them. What we do know is that clothes are functional and for many of us looking smart or chic or simply sharing a common identity with those with whom we want to belong is a way of giving individual or group expression to that functionality.

Inclusive education has its origins in debates between academics and in the emerging politics of disability which questioned the construction of 'normality' through the everyday interactions of cultural, social, economic and institutional life. In the face of an increasingly monolithic special education sector that primarily served the needs of twentieth-century mass education by isolating and removing from the mainstream those children who disrupted the assembly line, the early developers and advocates of inclusive education challenged the fundamentals of modern education. The critiques that underpinned inclusive education were focused not on children with special educational needs but on the mainstream education system. It was argued that mainstream systems of education established 'norms' that served to reinforce conformity in the modern world. Systems for the demarcation and institutionalization of 'failure', 'inadequacy' and 'disaffection' are products of nineteenth and twentieth-century systems of mass production. The 'inclusive' critique of special education has essentially been a critique of education as mass production.

The irony of the inclusive education critique is that it has been unable to build a socio-political base from which to challenge seriously the social interests that underpin modern systems of educational production, especially in the developed world. For this reason the analogy with fashion is correct. The success of haute couture depends upon translation into production, not upon a radical rethinking of the processes of production themselves. Indeed the sweatshops are its lifeblood. They feed the industry that makes haute couture not only possible but meaningful. In other words ideas operate within a context that makes their realization possible only within certain parameters. Ideas can challenge those parameters, and such challenges can contribute to change but they do not make change except on those rare occasions when they align with broader social upheavals. Thus, in the developed world at least, we have seen the haute couture of inclusion translated into the high street of policy and practice where they continue to keep the wheels of the existing system turning smoothly. At their crudest, they are copied in ways that dress up the existing systems of segregation and exclusion with the rhetoric of reform. At their best they disrupt and challenge everyday practices and suggest possibilities for new forms of social relations, new ways of understanding difference, new ways of valuing humanity. But fundamental change in the way in which education is organized and the purposes it serves has always been at the core of the inclusive education movement, and with respect to this we will argue that in the developed world the inclusive movement has been distorted, colonized and reinscribed by the traditional purpose of special education as a system for managing potential disruptions to the smooth flow of educational production.

This may seem to be a pretty depressing picture. Not entirely so we will argue. But for the inclusive ambition to be recaptured it is necessary to reassert its critique of mainstream education. In this respect there are real possibilities, not least because in the developed world the purpose of education is being rethought in so many fora. Traditional forms of schooling are themselves questionable in terms of the more fluid, globally interactive world in which we live. Opportunities for learning are to be found well beyond the traditional classroom. Also the mass production of human skills is no longer relevant in the same way as it once was, or at the very least the nature of the skills, attributes and identities which are valued (and the social mechanisms through which such valuing takes place). Education has the potential to be transformed through the enhanced opportunities for interaction that now exist. The closed social systems of class, gender and ethnicity which have been reproduced and reinforced by educational policy and practice in the service of nineteenth and twentieth-century modes of industrial production are increasingly outdated and irrelevant in today's world. Yet in saying this we should not forget that for many millions of children in the world there are no accessible educational services at all, and the sharp contrast between universal but outdated systems in the richer parts of the world and the complete absence of education in the most impoverished parts of the world is just as striking and as horrifying as the extreme differences in wealth and poverty that characterize our human community.

If we turn to the developing world we see an even more complex picture in relation to ideas of social inclusion and inclusive education. First, it needs to be recognized that the everyday experiences of people in the developing world are marked by the history of colonialism. The end of the colonial period towards the end of the twentieth century certainly did not eradicate the impact of that domination. In the post-colonial world those countries start from a position of economic disadvantage. They frequently lack the resources, the infrastructure and, as their educated children leave for highly paid jobs in the North, they so often also lack the skills base and leadership to challenge the new world order. Global power remains firmly in the hands of the former colonial powers. Even countries such as China, who clearly are driving forward on to the world stage through their economic revolution, have some way to go before they will match the advantages of the developed countries of the world.

Education as a commodity for export is nothing new. Colonial education systems have largely been built upon models taken from the colonial powers, and little has changed in the post-colonial world. The yoke of colonialism has perhaps been replaced by the 'aid' dollar, but a yoke it so often remains. Debt, the distortion of national educational priorities and the imposition of neo-liberal educational fads, each have characterized educational development in the post-colonial era. The transfer of ideas from the North to the South has been commonplace. Sometimes this transfer is based upon an intellectual colonialism which sees innovation and reform grounded in the schools systems of the North translated into the schools of Africa, Asia and Latin America. Often this has been promoted by funding agencies in the North who use educational reform as a vehicle for driving broader social and economic reconstruction, in recent times in particular around the decentralization and marketization of education. At other times we see a more benevolent intervention from educators from the developed world, as is the case with the use of the *Index for Inclusion* developed in the UK by Mel Ainscow and Tony Booth and widely used as a tool for supporting whole-school change in both the developed and developing worlds. The latter may bring some improvements in educational practice but such approaches hardly challenge the balance of power in respect of education and its outcomes between the North and the South. More home-grown initiatives, such as that developed in inclusive education by local special educators together with the teachers union in Trinidad and Tobago in the 1990s, described in Chapter 9 of this book, suggest more empowering processes of change and could provide the political impetus from which interventions around the *Index for Inclusion* could have more scope to contribute towards system-level changes.

The countries of the developing world have also been far more radical in their conceptualization of inclusive education than is generally found among the countries of the North. Operating through the agencies of the United Nations, educators from the South have led a movement to expand understanding of inclusion. They have, in particular, conceptualized inclusion in terms of the role of education in relation to poverty reduction, gender equality and social and economic development. There are many challenges facing these educators, not least that of confronting the continuing dependency on the North that these policy changes require if they are to have successful outcomes. Mass education systems in the South now produce workers in the developing world with the basic skills necessary to support cheap mass production for the North. But educational opportunity also creates new spaces for developing countries and, in particular, local educators' and teachers' organizations, to take ownership of the development agenda for their own countries.

In this book we set out to challenge some of the directions that inclusive education has taken, both in policy and practice. Our critique examines inclusive education in the developed world and in the developing world. A lot of what has been written, and the great majority of the research in this area, has focused on the developed countries of the North. Our view is that one of the outcomes of globalization over the past 50 or so years is that education systems across the world are interconnected and that to fully understand the development of education and its relation to the broader society, international interconnectedness needs also to be understood. Yet this is not a relationship of equals. Power, both political and economic, is not distributed evenly across the world. Educational policy and practice in developing countries continue in many ways to be framed by the broader relations between countries in the geopolitical world. So often educational policy is 'grown' in the developed world and exported in due course to developing countries. But in each case the local context of policy and practice allows us to examine the particular pressures for change within national education systems and the tensions that they can give rise to both nationally and internationally.

The structure of the book

In Chapter 1 we explore key issues that are framing current debates worldwide about inclusive education and, in particular, we introduce a developing world perspective on the study of inclusive education, a perspective that has commonly been disregarded in much that is written on inclusive education.

In Chapter 2 we step back from current developments to consider the history of special education out of which the movement for inclusive education has arisen. We argue that a form of inclusion in the sense of assimilation to a common identity (the identity of a workforce for mass production) characterized the education systems of the nineteenth and twentieth centuries in the developed world. However, in the transition from industrial to post-industrial systems of education in the North a new space for thinking about inclusive education systems has arisen. This reflects and emphasizes the uncertainty with regard to purpose and outcomes expected from education in the North. Yet the traditional drivers of educational production clearly operate to contain fundamental change and to re-create inclusive forms of education within more traditional modes of operation.

Chapter 3 brings us to reflect on the current state of inclusive education. We consider different definitions of inclusion and discuss the slippery nature of this concept in an attempt to move from the rhetoric to a deeper understanding of problems to which inclusive education is seen as being the answer. In the end it might be argued that inclusive education means all things to all people, but we argue that it can equally mean nothing and that this dilemma reflects both differences of perspective and intent among advocates of inclusion as well as tensions within education systems in the developed world where uncertainty of purpose in social and economic terms is causing loss of policy focus.

Education systems in the developing world face challenges around inclusion that for developed countries have largely been overcome many years ago, namely, basic access and participation. The United Nations policy of Education for All (EFA) has been a major focus for thinking in the South about inclusive education. With over 100 million children lacking basic access to education the scale of the challenge is immense, but in facing this challenge the developing world faces also the dual burden of support and control that emanates from the funding prescriptions of the North, from where much of the investment resource is controlled. Chapter 4 describes the history of the EFA movement, its challenges and constraints in promoting inclusion through education.

Chapter 5 examines case studies of sponsored interventions by United Nations policy agencies and international funding agencies into educational development in countries of the South. Chapter 6 looks at the European Union. Here we have seen significant rhetoric around inclusion as the nations of Europe have sought greater integration, founded upon the idea of the importance of social cohesion. However, in the educational sphere not only does there continue to be considerable difference and even fragmentation between national education systems, but also the idea of a common European identity struggles to find meaning within the new

Europe. Chapter 7 takes us to England for a detailed critique of the absorption of inclusive educational rhetoric into national policy for special education. In England, we argue, we have seen a classic case of the reconstruction of a special education system in the clothes of an inclusive rhetoric. This is not to deny that there have been major steps towards inclusive schooling in some areas but the broader framework within which educational policy sits is one that by its nature exclusively emphasizes outcomes that inhibit the development of a truly inclusive school practice.

We now turn to the question 'what future does inclusion have?'. We consider the ways in which policy has been translated into practice and how this has impacted upon the ways in which schooling is experienced for students and for teachers. In Chapter 8 we argue that the inclusive potential of an approach to education depends on whether it represents an orchestrated attempt to make schools more inclusive or whether it is primarily a way of managing students by minimizing disruption in regular classrooms. The question of how schools can become more inclusive cannot be seen in isolation from the question of whether the educational systems in which they are located are becoming more inclusive. Chapter 9 looks at the ways in which models of inclusive educational practice have been 'exported' to the South and discusses both the consequences of this for the development of local educational practice and the ways in which resistance to educational colonialism can transform practice within school systems in the South. In Chapter 10 we draw together the conclusions from our examination of the inclusive education phenomenon. In an epilogue we also take the opportunity to reflect on the themes of this book from the personal experience each of us as had in dealing with these issues over our careers in education.

Throughout the book we set out to engage the reader by identifying key discussion questions for each chapter and providing opportunities to explore case studies and guided reflection on our topic. At the end of each chapter are suggestions for specific reading for those who wish to follow up these issues with more in-depth study.

The term 'disabled people' is used in this book. 'Disabled people' is the preferred term for the social model of disability since it acknowledges that people are disabled by the environment, attitudes and stereotypes. We recognize that for readers in some countries the 'person first' concept is considered more appropriate but in making our choice of language, we hope that the book will contribute to this debate on the language of disability and inclusion.

A note on authorship

This book is the product of a collaborative process. Each of the authors took a lead in developing the major themes of the book across the three sections and responsibility for drafting particular chapters. However, this book reflects a collective understanding and common position built upon our work together over the past 10 years.

Acknowledgements

We wish to acknowledge the importance of the work of the University of Sheffield's Inclusive Education group, which brought us together, the support of the University of Sydney, which has allowed us to continue our collaboration, and the contribution to our thinking of our students from across the world.

We also wish to acknowledge the support of our parents for making any of this possible: Beryl and O'Hanley, Doris and Peter, and Katerina and Yiannis.

Section 1

History, Social Context and Key Ideas

In the first section of this book we discuss the history and social context of inclusive education and the relationship of this idea to systems of special education that grew up in the late nineteenth and twentieth centuries. We also explore broader concerns and debates about social justice, the rights of disabled people and 'education for all' that gained ground in educational thinking in the latter part of the twentieth century. More recent theories and perspectives on inclusive education are introduced and critiqued.

1

Inclusive Education: Key Themes

Chapter overview

This first chapter of our book sets out the central themes that we will be developing in later chapters. We pose the question: 'Does the idea of inclusive education amount to anything more than the vacuous theorizations of postmodernism on the one hand or the reframing of traditional policies for the management of troublesome children on the other hand?' In other words, is the idea of inclusive education an illusion? We argue that despite the idealism that characterized the origins of the inclusive education movement, its meaning in theory and policy is ambiguous and in practice its implementation has been limited. Yet, educational policy and practice are highly contested in different local contexts and it is in these contextualized struggles over the values and purposes of education that hope lies. We conclude by sketching out some ideas for rethinking the inclusive education project framed by the broader relationships between the contested values of education and the practical possibilities for making a difference.

Setting the scene

Worldwide, social inclusion has become a major focus of the policies of governments. Education reform is generally seen as a key driver for achieving social integration and cohesion. Until fairly recently, the separation between 'mainstream' schooling and 'special education' rested upon the idea of separate kinds of education for different kinds of children. Increasingly these categorical distinctions have been challenged. In part, this challenge has arisen from growing recognition of the broad continuum of human needs and the inadequacy of models that constrain educational possibilities by imposing different systems of schooling on those who are in some sense believed to be 'abnormal' or, to use a euphemism, 'special' (even where the intention is ultimately to foster greater integration into the mainstream system of schooling and/or society). Opposition to traditional systems of special education has often been led by disabled people and their supporters who have argued that 'special education' restricts opportunities for disabled people as citizens because of the way in which it labels them as having intellectual, social and/or physical deficits. In addition to these arguments, education policy-makers have also become interested in wider issues of social inclusion and how education might play a significant role in promoting social cohesion in societies that are increasingly diverse, socially and culturally. These ideas are to be found not just in the developed countries of North America, Europe and Australasia. In the developing world, too, considerable interest has been shown in the idea of 'inclusive education'. International agencies such as the United Nations and the United Nations Educational, Scientific and Cultural Organization (UNESCO), the World Bank and the UK's Department for International Development have been powerful advocates of 'inclusion' as a core principle of schooling and education systems.

In this book we examine the development of these new ideas about 'inclusive education' and their relationship to broader social policies aimed at promoting social inclusion. We argue in particular that:

- the idea of 'inclusive education', although historically closely related to debates and reforms in the field of special education, actually goes well beyond special education in its approach to social integration;

- inclusive education should be understood in the context of an approach to the 'problems' of social diversity which are the outcome of social changes since the end of the Second World War and which include the end of colonialism, the increase of labour-force mobility, and the tension between global and local cultures;

- there are continuing contradictions between policy and practice as education systems attempt to manage the social and economic complexities of national and cultural identity in societies that are highly diversified internally and yet globally interconnected;

- the growth of 'inclusive education' in the developing world in part reflects the attempt of these countries to promote the social and educational advantages of access to schooling and educational resources, and in part reflects the export of first-world thinking to countries which reinforces dependency and what Paulo Friere called 'the culture of silence'.

What is meant by 'inclusion'?

The meaning of 'inclusion' is by no means clear and perhaps conveniently blurs the edges of social policy with a feel-good rhetoric that no one could be opposed to. What does it really mean to have an education system that is 'inclusive'? Who is thought to be in need of inclusion and why? If education should be inclusive, then what practices is it contesting, what common values is it advocating, and by what criteria should its successes be judged? The introduction of these policies to education systems both in the countries of the North and in the 'developing countries' of post-colonial globalization is underpinned by a complex and contested process of social change. While social policy is dominated by the rhetoric of inclusion, the reality for many remains one of exclusion and the panacea of 'inclusion' masks many sins.

Inclusion and the politics of disability

The history of special education in Europe, North America and Australasia throughout the twentieth century was a history of expansion: growth in the number of children identified as having special educational needs, growth in the number of categories of 'handicap' or 'impairment' and growth in the number of schools outside the mainstream for children whose needs were seen as different to those of 'normal' children. In these countries, however, the concept of special educational needs was never simply synonymous with 'impairment'. Few children identified as having 'special educational needs' would later as adults be recognized as being 'disabled' and the terms 'impairment' and 'disability' were hardly ones that would resonate with the experiences of most children in special schools. There is little overlap between educational categories of special education need and generally much more narrow categories of disability or impairment used in the management of resources and identities in the adult world. Most children in special education have tended to be labelled as having learning difficulties or behavioural problems but these are labels with little scientific, let alone educational, credibility.

Nonetheless, the label of special educational needs plays a significant role in extending to a much greater number of people an educational rationale for failure within the educational system and the subsequent social marginalization and denial of opportunities that follows for those who are unsuccessful within the ordinary school system. In this way the disability discourse is seen by Fulcher as deflecting attention 'from the fact that it is failure in the education apparatus by those whose concern it should be to provide an inclusive curriculum, and to provide teachers with a sense of competence in such a curriculum, which constructs the politics of integration' (Fulcher, 1989: 276).

The concept of special educational needs is embedded in the trinity of social class, gender and race. The importance of these factors and indeed the social processes implicated in their application, have been well described by sociologists from at least the 1970s onwards (for example, Tomlinson, 1981, 1982). Yet the label continues to be used in ways that mask the intersection and operation of these factors in the identification of those with special educational needs in the daily decision-making of policy-makers and practitioners across the world. As many writers have argued it is only by examining these wider social relationships that insight is possible into the role of special educational needs as a discourse of power and its abuses.

In the developed world, the idea of 'inclusive education' is one that has challenged the traditional view and role of special education. This challenge has been significantly driven by the disabled people's movement in the UK, the USA and in Europe. It has fundamentally questioned policies and practices that have promoted segregation and 'human improvement', which have their origins in the eugenics movement and the social Darwinism of the late nineteenth and first half of the twentieth centuries. In place of eugenics, the disability movement has advanced a model of 'inclusive education' that is linked to a broader campaign for social justice and human rights.

That policy in this area continues to be contested is evident in the experience of a number of developed countries. In the UK, for example, the policy of inclusion has become a central plank of government reform since 1997. On the other hand, the radical ideas about social justice that characterized the development of inclusion as a political agitation by the disabled people's movement have largely been lost within the technical approaches to inclusive education that framed those policy applications in the UK in the narrower terms of 'school improvement', diversity of provision for different needs and academic achievement (Armstrong, 2005).

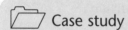 Case study

Greece: a policy case study

In Greece, the *renaming* of 'special classes' to 'inclusive classes' was one of the ways that education policy responded to the impetus of inclusion (Law 2817/2000). In the same legislation that introduced the name of 'inclusive classes', a complex bureaucratic assessment and evaluation process for the identification of students with a disability was put into place. This process reinforced the dominance of the 'medical model' in the education system by requiring children and young people to be 'labelled' with one of the recognized categories of disability before educational provision in the form of resources, additional support and instructional differentiation could become available. In practice, inclusive classes have continued in most cases to perform their role as 'withdrawn rooms' were students spend significant periods of their school time. This model 'regulates' the management of a part of the school population and 'avoids "contaminating" the mainstream educational praxis with "special education intervention or differentiation"' (Zoniou-Sideri et al., 2006: 285).

The dominance of a 'deficit model' in the Greek context is reinforced in the new Law. Despite the recognition that 'disability constitutes a natural part of the human condition' (Law 3699/2008, article 1, point 1), the dominance of a deficit approach is evident in the statement that 'the type and degree of special educational needs defines the form, kind and category of Special Education provision' (Law 3699/2008, article 2, point 1).

In the developing world as in the developed world inclusive education is used in quite different ways that mean different things. Sometimes it is framed in terms of social justice, such as where it is directly linked to the UNESCO's Education for All policy. In this reading an advocacy position is at the heart of the inclusive model. Translated into particular national settings within the developing world, inclusive education may in practice be a useful policy option that is less resource intensive than other approaches to the provision of services for disabled children. A more wide-ranging critique, however, might point to the context of exceptionally low achievement and the failure of educational systems in the developing world to address adequately the needs of the majority of a country's population. In this respect the language of 'inclusion' mirrors the role of the language of special education in Europe and North America from the late eighteenth century onwards as those systems sought to manage the 'flotsam and jetsam' created by a system of mass schooling. On the other hand, it is important to examine the reasons for system failure as these are often related to a combination of limited resources and the external manipulation of educational policy by external funding agencies pursuing agendas arising in the developed world. This places the notion of inclusion in highly contested political territory.

The politics of inclusive education

To appreciate the complex history that underpins the development of inclusive education, as both a political and a policy/practice discourse, a discussion of the meaning and significance of 'inclusion' in global educational practice today must be made concrete. For instance, in the newly globalizing discourse of inclusion, its radical humanistic philosophical premises should be placed in the more sobering context of the intersection between colonial histories and post-colonial contexts of countries in the developed and developing world (for example, by contrasting its rhetorical stance towards social cohesion with its practical limitations, or even complicity, in the management of diversity and, in particular, racial and cultural diversity in the interests of social hegemony, both nationally and internationally).

Similarly, the technological advances of the twenty-first century, the global-ization of economic markets and the penetration of 'first-world' knowledge and policy solutions into the developing world all may be understood as spreading an evangelical belief in the inclusion of diversity. Alternatively globalization and its impact on conceptualizations of inclusion may be understood in terms of a technical rationalism which has separated social practice from ethical thinking in the management of global social inequality. The precarious position of developing country economies, starved of invest-ment, historically constrained (internally as well as externally) by the baggage of colonialism, and economically disenfranchised by the political dominance of first-world countries, their donor agencies and the interests of multina-tional companies, is commonly reflected in both the need to develop human capital alongside economic investment and the inability of these countries to lift themselves out of disadvantages that are structural, global and embedded in the historical and cultural legacy of colonialism. Within this context, the exhortations of first-world aid agencies and international donors for countries to adopt inclusive education as a policy prescription to address both system failure and individual disadvantage can seem idealistic, if not patronizing and victimizing. On the other hand, the discourse of inclusive education can pro-vide a political space for contesting the wider agenda of social injustice. Here, as for example is the case with the promotion of 'inclusive education' by the member states of UNESCO, there are opportunities for advancing a progres-sive educational agenda that goes beyond the rhetoric of exhortation and the limitations of policy borrowing from first-world nations.

The globalizing discourse of inclusion

These contrasting agendas are evident in the competing policy frameworks that address issues of internationalization in educational policy. For instance, one of the most significant events of the twenty-first century has been the adoption by the United Nations General Assembly on 13 December 2006 of the *Convention on the Rights of Persons with Disabilities* which came into effect on 3 May 2008. The Convention does not explicitly define disability but it recognizes that 'disability is an evolving concept and that disability results from the interaction between persons with impairments and attitudinal and environmental barriers that hinders their full and effective participation in society on an equal basis with others' (UN, 2006: 1).

In the area of education, Article 24 of the Convention says that 'States Parties recognize the right of persons with disabilities to education. With a view to realizing this right without discrimination and on the basis of equal opportu-nity, States Parties shall ensure an *inclusive education system* at all levels and life-long learning' (UN, 2006: 16, emphasis added). In calling on states to ensure that 'effective individualized support measures are provided in environments that maximize academic and social development, consistent with the goal of full inclusion' (UN, 2006: 17), the Convention reinforces the centrality of inclusion in educational debates.

However, other considerations may have an equal if not greater bearing upon policy formulation and implementation in practice. For example, the United Nations *Standard Rules on the Equalization of Opportunities for Persons with Disabilities* (United Nations, 1993: 'Rule 6 of 22') recognized that special schools may have to be considered where ordinary schools have not be able to make adequate provisions. The focus on an 'inclusive education system' of the Convention on the Rights of Persons with Disabilities questions the 'necessity' of a segregated special education system. The tensions between an education system 'consistent with the goal of full inclusion' and a 'deficit approach' to education provision, in which the 'type and severity' of disability becomes the primary measure of access to a regular setting are more than obvious.

These tensions may play out differently in developed and developing countries. For example, the World Bank, which works in conjunction with the United Nations to provide loans to developing countries, has argued in favour of inclusion, justifying this position on the basis of the savings that integrated in-class provision offers compared with the prohibitive cost of segregated special education.

The financial incentives lying behind calls for the introduction of inclusive education are of great importance, since, as Tomlinson (1982: 174) argued 'it certainly will be cheaper to educate children with special needs in ordinary rather than special schools'. It is not only disabled people who are to be included in this category. For the most part, these are children who are experiencing difficulties with learning, rather than children with physical, sensory or learning impairments. The cost-effectiveness aspect of inclusive education is reiterated in the international organizations policy and documents. In UNESCO's (2005) *Guidelines for Inclusion*, the reference to the cost-effectiveness of inclusive education is supplemented with concerns about the privatization of inclusive education which may lead to 'cost-cutting' in areas that are essential if access to education for all is to be achieved.

Yet, increasingly the discourse of special education is being drawn upon to frame discussions and policy concerning educational failure. This illustrates a dilemma, not restricted to developing countries, but acutely experienced in these settings. On the one hand, the need for improved and targeted learning support coupled with the training of teachers, particularly in the mainstream sector, to work effectively with children with a range of special educational needs is very evident. On the other hand, the language of special education can itself impede an analysis of more deep-seated problems in respect of both funding and policy for improving the quality of education for all children.

The reality is that the goals of equity and equality of opportunity remain distant for many people in the developing world. For example, those stricken by poverty often experience academic deceleration and acquire special educational needs as they pass through the school system, leading to their eventual exclusion from those sections of the school system that offer the greatest prospects for upward social mobility.

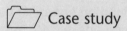 Case study

The Eastern Caribbean: a policy case study

The past 50 years has seen significant change in the countries of the Eastern Caribbean states with most of them gaining political independence, mostly from Britain, and thus experiencing tremendous change in their social and economic standing. The economic consequences of the collapse of the banana industry have impacted on family life, with many people of working age leaving the country to earn a living in the USA. This has seen the emergence of 'barrel children'; that is, children who are rolled backwards and forwards between the Caribbean and developed countries, both for socio-economic and family needs. Also, there has been an increase in the number of persons with HIV AIDS, including a growing school-age population with this condition. These countries were not prepared for such rapidly changing social and economic circumstances. One outcome has been an increase of the number of children in the region classified as having special educational needs as this label is conveniently used both to signify the effects of broader social and economic change and as a mechanism for dealing with the social and individual difficulties that arise from the impact of these broader social changes.

Yet, developments in special education and, more recently, inclusion have not been entirely planned and very often aid has been sought from diverse organizations with money tied to the donor policies and priorities of developed countries rather than a sound analysis of the needs of recipient countries. Special educational services and provision have therefore developed in fairly arbitrary ways within these islands.

A view from post-colonial theory

Homi Bhabha (1994) has argued that a view of global cosmopolitanism has emerged founded on ideas of progress that are complicit with neo-liberal forms of governance and free-market forces of competition. It is a cosmopolitanism that celebrates a world of plural cultures as it moves swiftly and selectively from one island of prosperity to another, 'paying conspicuously less attention to the persistent inequality and immiseration produced by such unequal and uneven development' (p. xiv). This 'one-nation' globalization is premised upon the assimilation of difference by an overriding imperative of technologically driven 'modernization'. This imperative, which has political and moral as well as economic dimensions, crosses boundaries that are both geographic and cultural. For example, the modernization project of New Labour in the reconstruction of the socio-economic landscape of Britain is at one with the post-colonial project by which developing countries are increasingly incorporated into the globalized world of free-trade and institutional homogeneity under the celebratory slogan of the inclusion of diversity. Yet in a most important sense globalization necessarily begins at home; in other words, with 'the difference within'. It is defined by the boundaries it places around inclusion; by the homogeneity of its view of diversity. Diversity is celebrated where it extends the reach of cultural dominance. Elsewhere, the opportunity to voice a different experience, a different reality, is closed down as is the case with indigenous peoples, for instance in Australia, whose land has been taken from them and whose cultures have been ridiculed, brutalized and reconstituted by colonial fantasies.

Implicit in much of the international policy on inclusion is an assumption that participation in education should be premised on the voices of young people being heard. This assumption, which has come to be accepted wisdom, is one that has arisen in a largely first-world literature. Little attention has been given in this literature on children's voices, a largely European and North American literature, to the ways in which participation is culturally specified through rites of passage and transition, and to the role and meaning of 'voice' in this process. Nor does it have much in common with the idea advocated by anti-colonial writers such as Paulo Freire who argued that colonialism imposed a 'culture of silence' which reinforced political domination and that resistance to colonization required a reclaiming of voice by colonized peoples.

The nature of research and development collaborations between special educators from first-world countries and developing countries, especially where the former are acting as change-agents often takes for granted concepts such as 'equity', 'social justice' and 'human rights', and in doing so abstracts them from the specific historical and cultural traditions of developing countries. Ironically, these concepts, which are introduced as guiding principles of education reform, mask the unequal and dependency promoting relationship between change-oriented development interventions sponsored by outside funding agencies and the recipients of such programmes. Thus, when policies on inclusive education are developed independently from consideration of the broader social context within which they are situated it is unlikely that they will be effective. More importantly, there is also a danger of limiting the very real possibilities for sharing experiences and educational thinking that do exist but which are dependent upon a very different notion of collaboration.

Summary

Many of the issues which have been identified in this chapter have arisen as a result of a legacy of the economic inequalities which developing countries have to manage in providing educational services. These inequalities are located in:

- the colonial heritage of developing countries;
- the continuing economic disadvantages experienced by developing countries compared to first-world nations;
- the domination in research and policy development of ideas arising out of the developed countries.

More recently, there have been international attempts to raise the profile of inclusive inclusion as a policy priority but the reality for developing countries is often one in which the international rhetoric of inclusion is experienced, ironically, as reinforcing the exclusion of entire peoples from economic and social opportunities.

In the countries of the North the idea of inclusion has frequently been framed almost exclusively by policy on school performance and measurable outcomes.

Retracing the development of inclusion back to the radical beginnings of the inclusion movement may help us to understand the potential of this movement as an educational reform project. As the important observation by Len Barton (2001: 10–11) emphasizes: 'inclusive education is not an end in itself, but a means to an end, that of the realisation of an inclusive society. Thus, those who claim to a commitment to inclusive education are always implicated in challenging discriminatory, exclusionary barriers and contributing to the struggles for an inclusive society'.

We also need to consider how this initial impetus has been reframed by quite different policy objectives within the developed and developing countries of the world and in the relationship between them.

Discussion questions

- Inclusive education is a feel-good idea, but what does it mean?
- Is inclusive education just another way of saying special education?
- Does inclusive education mean the same thing in the world's developing countries as it does in the developed countries of Europe and North America?
- What has been the significance of the history of colonialism, and now globalization, on the development of thinking about 'inclusive education' in the developing world?

Further reading

Bhabha, H. (1994) *The Location of Culture*. London: Routledge.

Fulcher, G. (1989) *Disabling Policies? A Comparative Approach to Educational Policy and Disability*. London: The Falmer Press.

Tomlinson, S. (1982) *A Sociology of Special Education*. London: Routledge.

UNESCO (1994) *The Salamanca Statement and Framework for Action on Special Needs Education*. Paris: UNESCO.

UNESCO (2005) *Guidelines for Inclusion: Ensuring Access to Education for All*. Paris: UNESCO.

2

The Social History of Inclusion

Chapter overview

The twentieth century was played out against the backdrop of wars, revolutions and the anti-colonial struggles of developing countries. More recently we have witnessed the growth of globalization. This history has shaped and inspired debates about education and social policy, reflecting struggles that have taken place around the meaning of citizenship and democracy. What does the way we organize our education systems tell us about the kind of society we live in and our aspirations for the future? Can we speak meaningfully of children's needs independently of social context, values and norms? In this chapter we consider the growth of special education as a product of mass education in Europe and North America in the late nineteenth and early twentieth centuries. Drawing on a case study of the UK we analyse the aspirations and struggles for control embodied in the development of a mass education system. Finally, we locate current debates (both about the ethics of social inclusion and the policy imperatives that frame educational reform) within the structures, controls and aspirations of the socio-political landscape of globalization.

Concerns about the education of young people are not new. In evidence to a committee of inquiry in 1840 (quoted by Lawson and Silver, 1973: 271) one witness maintained that: 'before the working classes … can be proof against the delusive seductions of socialism far more extended and energetic efforts must be made to improve them. They must not merely be schooled but educated'. However by 1897 a London School Inspector could still report that 'out of every seventy children, twenty-five were entirely ignorant, they misbehaved, learned nothing and truanted' (quoted in Pritchard, 1963: 117). Eighty years later, the UK's Secretary of State for Education, Sir Keith Joseph, suggested that 40 per cent of children impeded the smooth running of the mainstream school.

Over the years education systems have increasingly provided explanations for social and economic inequality. The education system may provide a vehicle for advancement within a meritocracy, but it also serves as a tool for defusing political dissent by promoting the idea that the privileged deserve their social position and rewards.

The transformation from pre-modern to modern times was characterized by the presence of a new tension between society and the individual and a new problem: the problem of how to maintain social order in the face of this tension between society and individual. On one side was a rational model of the social world in which a natural order of progress was believed to be unfolding which would lead to the assimilation of differences in a society characterized by a common purpose. On the other side the very idea of civil society was rejected and replaced with a belief in the independent authority of individual reason. Individualism not only created diversity but required it. These two responses to the modern world gave rise to two very different approaches to education. Social and educational policy from one perspective was concerned with compensation and assimilation, from the other it was concerned instead with the policing of moral boundaries and risk management.

The question of how to secure a stable social order within which diversity could flourish as a catalyst for renewal was to become a central concern of modernity. Rationalism provided modern society with both the means of its realization and the mechanism for controlling the unpredictability of the social diversity that threatened to undermine it. A rational conception of humanity implied both the exclusion of irrationalism from human affairs together with the possibility of rehabilitation, treatment or correction. In pursuit of these dual ends the specification of difference through observation, classification and regulation quickly became the hallmarks of modernity.

Zygmunt Bauman (1990) has argued that what is distinctively modern is the concern with order and the fear that unless some action is taken, order will dissipate into chaos. Yet, Bauman also argued that this rationalist ideal is not only an impossible ambition to realize but also highlights the contradiction which 'resides in the very project of *rationalization* inherent in modern society' between society and the individual.

Assimilation and the policy contradictions of education

A belief in the rational ordering of the world and therefore in the possibility of manipulation of the world by rational action, increasingly informed an interventionist social policy agenda during the nineteenth and twentieth centuries. The 'vigilant management of human affairs' focused upon the identification and classification of those human attributes that threatened the rational model of 'man'. Yet, in identifying and classifying these attributes, the aim was not to cast those who held them out of society. Unlike the leper colony of the pre-modern world, and the 'ship of fools' (Foucault, 1967) at the beginning of the modern world, the chaos that threatened the rational ordering of things was to be disarmed, treated and assimilated within the realm of reason. Education became centrally concerned with the management and assimilation of a chaotic and delinquent population of youth.

Thus, modernism was based upon an assumption of a society that both defined the parameters of rational behaviour and sought to neutralize or absorb difference through mechanisms of inclusion. Exclusion occurred not as a central defining process of social relationships but operated on the margins of the accepted social order. It was a mechanism for managing chaos that *for the moment* could not be understood and could not be rehabilitated within the prevailing social order. Exclusion represented an admission of the failure of the project of modernity and for that reason the violence of its response could be extreme. The thrust of the modernist project was towards assimilation. Social progress was embodied in the successful incorporation of difference within a reality that was fairly homogenous and therefore unchaotic.

The assimilation project of modernity extended across all areas of social life. It formed, for example, a cornerstone of the policy of empire. Similarly, it was central to the introduction and expansion of a system of universal education towards the end of the nineteenth century. The 'chaos' of national and tribal differences were assimilated into the order of empire in just the same way as working-class youth (demonized for the 'chaos' and disorder of their lives) were assimilated into socially useful labour by the inclusivity of the factory and the school.

Throughout the twentieth century, education was at the cutting edge of the modernist project of assimilation. The refinement of procedures for testing and measuring children's abilities and performance created possibilities for maximizing the effectiveness of schooling as a system for maintaining social control and perpetuating social roles and rewards.

Post-war reform in England: a case study

The years following the end of the Second World War witnessed wide-ranging social reform. Education was at the centre of the reform movement. Education was a key to change in society, both for reformers who saw it as the catalyst and vehicle for realizing the aspirations of the masses, and for those at the forefront of the new economic revival who saw it as the means of preparing a skilled and motivated workforce.

Post-war educational reform can be understood as an attempt to engineer a society in which the needs of all citizens were addressed through schools which were designed to meet their different needs. Society may be highly differentiated but, the engineering of social reform continued to be framed by the boundaries of a homogeneous social order. Each person has a place and knows where that place and its boundaries are. Education, rather than excluding the child from participation in society, in fact located the child and provided opportunities within society, yet this process of inclusion did nothing to challenge the nature of this social order as one within which diversity must be assimilated and therefore controlled.

The 'inclusive' character of these reforms is suggested by what McCulloch (1994: 93) in a discussion of educational reform in England described as 'education as a civic project'. McCulloch argues that the 1944 Education Act was the 'high water mark' of this project, represented as a means of securing equality of opportunity and, by furthering social cohesion, enhancing the role of citizenship.

However, McCulloch goes on to argue that although the reforms of the 1940s pursued a strongly civic goal, they lacked the means to achieve this goal. The tripartite divisions of 'academic', 'technical' and 'vocational' education that lay at the heart of the 1944 Act created a new hierarchical typology of citizenship.

That the 1944 *Education Act* was a compromise, and a compromise that diverted the education policy agenda away from a transformatory politics, has been widely argued. Tawney (1952: 144), for example, had argued that: 'The English educational system will never be one worthy of a civilized society until the children of all classes in the nation attend the same schools.' Yet, the introduction of compulsory post-elementary education established the principle that all children are educable and therefore that their educational needs should be met within the school system. Although laying the foundations for separate forms of education for different types of child, in another respect there was clear evidence of inclusive thinking within this legislation. The Act introduced the principle of 'education for all'. However in conceptualizing universal education in terms of a differential understanding of children's 'academic', 'technical' and 'vocational' educational 'needs', and therefore ultimately their place in society, the tripartite system was incapable of challenging the hierarchies of social and economic power and privilege embedded within the education system and within the wider society. The expansion of a fourth stream of separate special education for those who could not manage in, or would not be managed by, the secondary modern sector, was similarly concerned with including all sections of the child population, even the most troublesome, within a single differentiated but interrelated system.

By the 1970s, there existed a large and costly system of special educational provision outside of the mainstream school sector that largely catered for 'troublesome' children with learning difficulties and behavioural problems. Yet, as Tomlinson's (1981) study of the assessment of children identified as 'educationally subnormal' showed, the procedures for categorizing educational needs in terms of 'handicap' were often the product of different and competing professional interests. Assessments tended to be based on assumptions that were rarely made explicit by professionals. These were derived from professionals' perceptions of their own roles and interests rather than from any 'objective' assessment of the child's needs. The system of categorization served in practice to reinforce the 'expertise' of professionals while operating as a bureaucratically convenient, if crude, mechanism for rationalizing the redistribution of resources encouraged by the civic project of the 1944 Act. Special education had assumed a logic of its own in which it simply served the interests of the mainstream sector by removing troublesome children and the interests of professional groups whose 'specialist' identities were legitimated by the continuing existence of the system.

The *Warnock Committee*, set up in 1974 in response to a growing disenchantment with the 1944 framework, was to have wide-ranging influence upon the subsequent development of special educational policy and practice. The report, for the first time, recognized schools as a context within which children's educational needs might be created. This is significant because it implies that the educational needs of a child may vary according to factors occurring within the school attended. The Warnock Report (DES, 1978) does need to be seen within the overall context of an attempt to construct a more rational framework for identifying and dealing with children failing in, or failed by, the mainstream school system.

The 'discovery' by the *Warnock Committee* of 18 per cent of children with 'special educational needs' within the mainstream school can be seen as reflecting concern about the academic failure of large numbers of children within the mainstream sector and a critique of the school system. On the other hand, it is hardly unimportant that this discovery was revealed in the wake of the raising of the school-leaving age to 16 and at a time when there was a growing crisis of youth unemployment accompanied by concerns about delinquency and social disaffection. In the context of an enforced extension of compulsory education for young people who neither wanted it nor benefited from it, together with restricted employment opportunities, the educational label of 'special needs' conveniently legitimated the educational and socio-economic disadvantages experienced by young people.

The *Warnock Committee* argued that 20 per cent of children would have special educational needs at some point in their school lives. What are the relative merits of the two set out interpretations below of the significance of the Warnock Report?

1. The *Warnock Report:*

   - attempted to construct a more rational framework for identifying and dealing with children failing in, or failed by, the mainstream school system;

   - recognized that special educational needs arose from the context of the child's experience which includes family life and the quality of schooling;

   - identified the presence of large numbers of children (18 per cent) in mainstream schools who were failing because their 'special educational needs' were not being address and led to significant improvement in their educational opportunities.

2. The *Warnock Report:*

   - conveniently legitimated the educational and socio-economic disadvantages experienced by young people;

   - embodied an ideology of individual failure (be it failure of the child or of the school);

   - inhibited discussion of 'inclusion' in the context of a wider political critique of the relationship between education policy and the social relations within society.

The regulation of failure

Regulation theorists have argued that the institutions of the state are underpinned by modes of regulation which institutionalize conflict and confine it within certain parameters compatible with the maintenance of social order. The intervention of the state in education thus became a central feature of state formation in the late nineteenth and early twentieth centuries. The social compromise of 1945 lay in the preservation of the dominant social values of the time through the creation of mechanisms to alleviate the social cost endemic in the incoherence of economic individualism. These mechanisms included the partial regulation of markets through the intervention of the state and the regulation of social disadvantage through the welfare state. Whereas liberal individualism had represented rights as asserted always in defence of private interests, welfare rights were acknowledged as legitimate claims on the state to support those people who were most disadvantaged by capitalist forms of production and distribution. However, the justification for such intervention was not primarily moral. Rather, it lay in attempts to correct and improve upon the market in order to optimize the allocation to choices through the 'Pareto principle', which maintains that improvements in the social condition of one individual which do not make others worse off are ethically neutral. The provision of welfare benefits is, in theory, a form of insurance to which all members of society potentially have access.

Needs theory has had a central place within the welfare rights discourse and has been a significant feature of the development of special education systems across Europe since 1945. There was an assumption that educational needs could be accurately assessed by reference to some assumed minimum or norm that then legitimated the redistribution of 'social' wealth. Significant deviations from the norm would be identified as indicative of 'special' needs requiring the allocation of compensatory resources. Thus, needs theory retained the focus upon the individual that was characteristic of pre-war liberalism while advocating the role of the state as the protector or guardian of citizens against the anarchy of private interests. The role of social democracy was to regulate competing individual interests while providing a cushion of support for those whose needs were marginalized by the social outcomes of this competition. This view of social democracy assumed, however, that the state is neutral. Yet such a representation is deeply problematic.

The society in which we live is one where production for profit remains the basic organizing principle of economic life requiring the disciplining of labour power to the purposes of capital accumulation. This in turn gives rise to contradictions in the regulatory role of the state in the social and economic life. The viability of the welfare state lay in the provision of a context that supported the accumulation of capital. However, welfare policies exposed the contradictions between the political role of the state in legitimating the accumulation of capital and the economic consequences for the capitalist system of the appropriation of surplus value by the state.

'Personal choice' and inclusive education

By the 1980s, a new era of financial deregulation and political individualism had begun to take hold, first, in Britain and North America and, then, spreading rapidly around the world. Thinking about education as a vehicle for advancing social justice gave way to 'personal choice' theories. These celebrated the rights of the individual and the role of education as a commodity to be traded in the marketplace and to be employed as social capital. This new discourse centred on the failure of schooling to meet the needs not only of their pupils but of the wider society and importance of the accountability of schools and teachers, both to their students and parents, and through them to the nation as a whole.

The birth of the 'audit society', in which accountability re-conceptualized the social purpose of schooling, opened the doors to cost–benefit analyses as the measure of educational outcomes and the value and effectiveness of schools. Ironically, it also pushed the 'inclusion debate' into the mainstream of policy pronouncements. A political programme for social and economic inclusion, centred upon the value of educational achievement in the marketplace, resurrected the human capital theory of education and training. Yet, it did little to challenge the inequalities that underpin the exclusion of those with limited exchange value in the marketplace of employment. Human capital theories of education do little to advance the interests of young people and adults with learning difficulties who are increasingly excluded from the labour market.

Moreover, the policy rhetoric of inclusion disguises the political and financial interests that control the extent to which goods and services are redistributed according to 'need'. In other words, the irony here may be that 'inclusive' education becomes the rhetoric that legitimates the withdrawal of an inclusive, if imperfect, system of social welfare.

Education systems are contextualized by their histories and the struggles that have formed and shaped their role, but they are also given meaning by aspirations for the future. In the modern world, education systems are central to the contestation of political and social values. Educators, as citizens, are participants in those struggles. In this process the meaning of democracy is emergent and evolving.

The crisis of purpose in education is a worldwide crisis, but it also reflects a wider process of redefinition of the character and role of the state. The neo-liberal critique of education claims that traditional, state-controlled systems have lacked both the flexibility and the will to respond imaginatively to the challenges of the new times in which we live. Education systems are seen as part of the bureaucracy of post-war welfare idealism gone wrong; one element in an egalitarian utopia that has atrophied, on the one hand, into a dependency creating system of pity and, on the other hand, into a system that stifles opportunity and initiative by the imposition of mediocrity. It is argued that public education no longer demonstrates 'fitness for purpose' because the purpose towards which it directs its energies is located in a world that no longer exists and is based on an ideology that is no longer relevant. What so animates neo-liberal politicians is their belief that the education system is holding society back while unproductively consuming considerable, potentially wealth-creating, resources.

The modern discourses of 'accountability' of 'standards' of 'choice and diversity', are central both to the re-conceptualization of purpose in education and to the management of youth through the school system. What we are witnessing is, in part, an attempt to rein-in what is seen as a burgeoning state bureaucracy. It is about a disinvestment in the state; a refusal to see the role of the state as being able to provide educational opportunities and support as a right. This reflects a belief in self-help as well as a belief that the state is a self-reproducing bureaucracy that diverts resources from the creative and wealth-producing sectors of society into systems of administration and welfare support that reinforce the dependency of the poor on those same bureaucracies. For neo-liberals this is not simply a commitment to the interests of the rich over the poor. Nor does it entail a lack of interest in the poor. It follows instead from the view that the position of the less advantaged is best improved by giving more entrepreneurial members of society the freedom to generate wealth which necessarily through increased employment opportunities will filter down to the less well off. The second strand to the neo-liberal argument, however, is that in breaking the dependency of low-income groups on welfare they too will become more entrepreneurial and wealth-generating members of society. What stands in the way of this goal is the state itself, or at least that element of the state bureaucracy that works against the interests of the market.

Yet the state, in fact, retains considerable power and authority within the neo-liberal world. As Andrew Gamble (1988) has argued, what has characterized modern government over the past three decades is the project of creating a free economy and a strong state; in other words, minimalist state involvement in the social sphere contrasting with a strengthening of the capacity of the state within the parameters of the authority that it continues to assert. This is evident in arenas of international affairs and internal security. Paradoxically, the power of the state is also evident within those very domains, such as education, that are attacked for their interference with the freedom of the market. In this respect the authority of the state is used to reduce the influence of those groups who stand outside the neo-liberal project – trade unions, teacher organizations, political opponents.

The centralization of power within the state apparatus increasingly involves the state in the regulation of its institutions and agencies while at the same time deregulating the context within which they operate. Diversity of provision is encouraged, private schools are advantaged over public schools and universities are deregulated and forced into self-privatization in the face of funding cuts and moves towards a free market for providers. Simultaneously, the state is busily enhancing its control over the declining public sector. Schools face greater regulation and control over what can be taught and how.

Education as a democratic practice

One of the biggest challenges facing us is that of developing a democratic practice based on a critical questioning of the contested social and political interests that inform educational policy and practice. To be critical is to take risks but it entails asking questions about whose interests are served by particular ways of conceptualizing educational value and practice. But questioning what the powerful would have us believe must be at the heart of the aspirations of a democratic society. To question the institutionalization of dominant ideas as scientific knowledge derived from the application of scientific method is to conceptualize the educational process as democratic but also to place those engaged in this work in a highly political realm. This is not to say that our own practice as educators should be ideological. Quite the reverse: it would be equally anti-democratic to simply oppose dominant ideas. The point is that education as a democratic activity involves critical dialogue with all ideas, practices and structures. This requires that the skills of dialogue be placed at the centre of the learning process. We shape our world in communion with our history. Learning always involves a revisiting and a reconstitution of the truth through critical dialogue.

It is important to ground an understanding of recent thinking and practice in the field of inclusive education in the historical context and, in particular, with reference to the expansion of special education in response to the introduction of mass systems of secondary education. Education systems designed to extend opportunities to all ironically face the problem of how to deal with those who cannot or will not learn within the 'normal' parameters of a mass system. For this reason there are two contradictory forces at work: one which is broadly inclusive and concerned with extending opportunities to all; another, concerned with establishing systems and processes to manage children who do not fit within the mainstream system. These early developments of national systems of special education were largely confined to the industrializing countries of the North in the nineteenth and early twentieth centuries. Although it is not uncommon to find examples of charitable schools for the disabled in the developing world during this period, systematic approaches to special education were absent because mass systems of education were not established to the same extent in these parts of the world.

During the latter half of the twentieth century traditional models of separate special education provision began to be widely questioned. There was criticism of special schooling on the grounds that it labelled people on the basis of a disability irrespective of a person's educational needs and abilities, and that this labelling process institutionalized discrimination against the disabled and reinforced discriminatory practices against minority groups and against the poor who were heavily over-represented among those labelled as having special educational needs. In addition, separate special education provision was also increasingly criticized for reasons of its costliness as the number of children being identified as having special educational needs continued to grow.

The *Warnock Report* in England was one response to this situation. This report attempted to frame special educational needs within the broader context of school, family and community rather than simply in terms of supposed individual deficits. It also conceptualized special educational needs as on a continuum that extended well into the mainstream through the identification of 18 per cent of children within that system as having learning difficulties. Ultimately the *Warnock Report's* approach to special education failed. In part, this was because it put forward a definition of special educational needs without any clear principles to guide resource allocation. More significantly it failed because its philosophy was grounded in a post-war model of welfarism that was about to be superseded by the neo-liberal philosophy of personal choices as the driving force for making schools and teachers accountable for the educational outcomes of their pupils.

The inclusive education movement in its origins was certainly informed by high ideals for a just and fair society and the abolition of systems and processes that ingrained disadvantage and discrimination through the limited availability of educational opportunities. Yet in the new political context of post-welfare neo-liberalism these ideals were transformed into more utilitarian arguments about the efficiency of schools, the measurement of outcomes and the accountability to consumers (parents and children). The inclusive philosophy of post-war education was replaced by a new 'inclusive' philosophy of the market and its ability to improve outcomes through the accountability of personal choice.

☐ Summary

Inclusive education has grown out of the system of special education that itself grew up in Europe, North America and other developed countries, during the nineteenth and twentieth centuries, as newly introduced mass education systems attempted to manage the learning of children who had a wide range of abilities, aptitudes and motivation. The aim of these mass education systems was to provide the basic education necessary for working-class factory and agricultural labourers, for the skilled factory workers of the industrial revolution, and for the growing commercial and professional middle classes. The creation of different schools for different types of child was an obvious solution to the broad question of what to teach. Those who were unable or unwilling to fit within the broad moulds of nineteenth-century educational mass production were increasingly accommodated in schools for the 'feebleminded' and 'maladjusted', later transformed into 'special schools' and 'special units'. This was in practice inclusive in that for the first time many children received an education, but its intention was to assimilate, that is, to make 'normal', as far as this was possible, those children who could not or would not fit into the ordinary school. In this chapter it has been argued that the history of special education has been a history of tension between assimilation and regulation, between inclusion on the one hand and segregation and control on the other. The inclusive education movement has presented major challenges to the traditional special education sector but as a child of the special education system it remains unclear whether it is really capable of 'leaving home'.

 Discussion questions

- What does the way we organize our education systems tell us about the kind of society we live in and our aspirations for the future?
- Can we speak meaningfully of children's needs independently of social context, values and norms?
- Consider the ways in which segregated and inclusive education approaches might be considered from different perspectives – a teacher, a parent, a student and a government policy-maker. What might the advantages and disadvantages be from each of these perspectives in judging the value of each approach to the education of a 'learning disabled' or a 'sensory impaired' student? How would you attempt to resolve possible differences of opinion on this issue?

Further reading

Armstrong, D. (2003) *Experiencing Special Education*. London: Routledge.

Armstrong, F. (2003) *Spaced Out: Policy Difference and the Challenge of Inclusive Education*. Dordrecht: Kluwer Academic. Chapter 4.

Barton, L. (2005) *Special Educational Needs: An Alternative look (A Response to Warnock M. 2005: Special Educational Needs – A New Look)*. Accessible at: www.leeds.ac.uk/disability-studies/archiveuk/barton/Warnock.pdf.

Thomas, G. and Loxley, A. (2001) *Deconstructing Special Education and Constructing Inclusion*. Buckingham: Open University Press.

Tomlinson, S. (1982) *A Sociology of Special Education*. London: Routledge and Kegan Paul.

Warnock, M. (2005) *Special Educational Needs: A New Look*. Macclesfield. Philosophy of Education Society of Great Britain.

3

The Current State of Inclusive Education: Contradictions and Concerns

Chapter overview

Observing the current state of inclusive education, it appears that the social justice underpinnings of inclusive education have failed for the most part to be translated into effective policies and practices. While educational systems continue to struggle to manage diverse student populations, inclusive education tends to be reduced to a new name for 'special education'. Even in cases where inclusive education is perceived as an opportunity for change, assumptions about normality and the normalization role of schools are not questioned and challenged.

Has inclusion turned into a 'soft' approach to dealing with populations that are increasingly perceived in terms of medical categories?

Is this conception of inclusion another way of reinforcing the dominance of the medical model of disability?

In this chapter we argue that the great expectations of the early 1990s have been replaced by a lack of critical engagement with the realities of education and schools. There is a theoretical vacuum reflected in the escapism of much of the postmodern writings on inclusion or in the pragmatic watering-down of the underlying idealism of inclusion.

In the previous chapter we outlined a number of issues that we consider central in understanding the development of inclusive education. Here we explore the complexities involved in understanding the significance of inclusive education and its implications for the current state of the field. These complexities can be considered under four broad headings.

- The complex diverse origins of the inclusive education movement.

- The problem of definition.

- The different modes of realization of inclusive education in policy and practice.

- The outcomes of inclusion.

The origins of inclusion

The early calls for inclusion in the mid-1980s and early 1990s emanated from different groups with different experiences. However, together they presented a powerful critique of existing and emerging issues in education. There were four different strands to this critique.

Parents, teachers and advocates of students with disabilities promoted inclusion as a way of challenging the restrictions to *access* and *participation* imposed by existing models of 'mainstreaming' or 'integration'. This critique disputed three main assumptions of existing policy and practice. First, that there is a threshold to the level of education that some students are able to access due to the type and/or severity of their disability. Second, that in order to meet effectively the distinct needs of students identified as having special education needs and disabilities, there must be a complex system of identification and assessment based on the attributes or behaviour of the individual child. Third, that special forms of provision for instruction are required, frequently necessitating removal of the child with special educational needs from the regular classroom for a substantial part of their school life. This critique was developed mainly in contexts where mainstreaming and integration were already established, such as in Northern America, England, Australia and New Zealand.

The development of social definitions of disability by disabled and non-disabled activists and theorists influenced the critique of the role of education, and special education in particular, in reproducing the exclusion and oppression of disabled people (Oliver, 1996). The *Social Model* of disability influenced relevant discussions and debates in inclusive education. According to the Social Model a person's impairment is not the cause of disability, but rather disability is the result of the way society is organized, which disadvantages and excludes people with impairments. It follows from this that the focus should not be on the person with an impairment and how they can be made to 'fit' into schools (individual model of disability), but rather on removing any barriers within schools that disable the person with an impairment. The discussions and debates within Disabilities Studies about the relation of impairment and disability also have implications for inclusive education, and its influence on thinking about inclusive education has been considerable.

Advocates of inclusive education mounted a challenge to the education reform programmes that were taking place in a number of countries and which introduced market-driven arrangements in schools, promoting specific notions of accountability, control, choice and diversity. Central to this discussion is the examination of how difference is managed within educational systems through the identification and labelling of individuals and groups, and through the interrelated processes of inclusion and exclusion.

Calls for inclusive education have become a significant feature of programmes for educational change in developing countries. While the work of international organizations has been instrumental in constructing inclusion as an international aim, we argue in this book that there has been little two-way exchange between the countries of the South and the North.

It can be argued that the power of inclusion as a critical project lies to its extensive focus. Inclusion generated a critique of special education that moved beyond a simple dichotomy of mainstream and special education. Although the practices and effectiveness of special education have been criticized, the main focus of critique has been on the purpose of special education as a separated but interlinked sub-system of education. Tomlinson (1982) demonstrated the ways that special education works to control the smooth working of general education, which is unable or unwilling to educate a significant minority of the school population. However, as we discussed in the previous chapter, the underpinning of this critique is based on specific values about education and the society that it serves. As Barton (1995: 157) argues, 'special education entails a discourse of exclusion and this is seen as a particularly offensive aspect of such provision'. Thus a values perspective that promotes social justice and equal participation in education and society cannot provide a justification for special education.

Even though special education needs are usually located on the perimeter of education, it is at this boundary where 'normality' in educational terms is defined. It is questionable that the inclusive education movement has really redefined what is viewed to be 'normal' but it has been successful in challenging the boundaries. For example, increasingly mainstream teachers are required (for example, by special education needs and disability legislation, their preparation courses, and teachers' accreditation bodies) to have the skills that will enable them to meet the diverse needs of their students, including students with disabilities and special education needs. Locating the inclusion debate within the general education context has been a substantial development in the past 20 years or so in many countries and cause for celebration for many students, their families and those who advocate for inclusion. However, the resistance of schools and teachers to embracing inclusion, the reasons informing this resistance, and the continuing perceptions of some groups of students as 'problems to be managed' remain causes for concern.

Defining inclusion

As inclusion gained currency in theoretical debates and policy programmes, the broad terms of 'inclusion', 'educational inclusion' and 'inclusive education' have accommodated diverse meanings. It is a common adage that *'inclusion means different things to different people'*. The difficulty of providing a definition of inclusion that describes inclusion in a positive way (that is, in terms of what it is rather than what it is not) is partly due to the complexity of its origins. For example, it is very common to find statements of the type: 'inclusion is not simply a different word for special education' or 'inclusion is not only about disabled students or students with special education needs'. Such statements can be represented as 'negative' definitions of inclusion, but in saying what it is not, no indication is given by these statements about what would actually change with the introduction of inclusive education. Some writers propose that it is preferable to talk about *inclusions* in the plural (Dyson, 1999) but this really avoids the issue by merely stating the obvious; namely, that the term is used in many different ways to mean different things.

Ironically, in the absence of any clarity about its meaning the rhetoric of inclusion in educational policy and practice has become ever more pronounced. An ever-expanding literature on the implementation of inclusive strategies and practices in the classroom has perhaps been the most concrete outcome of the inclusion movement. Important as these are, they hardly fulfil the promise of the inclusion movement for making significant systems-level change.

The reality is not simply that inclusion means different things to different people, but rather that inclusion may end up meaning everything and nothing at the same time. We have suggested that in its origins the argument for inclusion provided a powerful critique of educational systems and current practice. In particular this critique emphasized the potential role of schooling in creating inclusive and democratic societies. Yet, in practice, this powerful insight has been largely diluted as it has struggled to spell out a clear set of principles and practices in the face of a rhetoric of convenience which embraces the 'feel-good' aspects of the inclusive discourse without serious engagement with the issues that it exposes in respect of the purposes and values of educational practice.

Ainscow et al. (2006) attempt to address this problem by distinguishing two types of definitions. According to them there are 'descriptive' definitions of inclusion, which specify the variety of ways 'inclusion' is used in practice. But there are also 'prescriptive' definitions, which indicate the way we intend to use the concept and would like it to be used by others. However, this distinction is not entirely clear since how inclusion is used in practice is not independent of how, for example, policy definitions prescribe inclusion. More useful for our discussion may be another distinction that Ainscow et al. (2006) make between 'narrow' and 'broad' definitions of inclusion. Narrow definitions of inclusion refer to the promotion of the inclusion of specific group of students, mainly but not exclusively disabled students and/or students with special education needs in 'mainstream' or 'regular' education. 'Broad' definitions of inclusion, on the other hand, do not focus on specific groups of students, but rather on diversity and how schools respond to the diversity of *all* students and every other member of the school community. We would also add another dimension to this distinction, which we can call 'fragmented' definitions. Both narrow and broad definitions can be fragmented when they break down the group that they refer to. This way of distinguishing definitions of inclusion can be helpful when looking at what exactly is being proposed by policy documents. For example, in the UK the Office for Standards in Education's *Guidance for Evaluating Educational Inclusion* (Ofsted, 2000: 7, emphasis added) states that:

> An *educationally inclusive school* is one in which the teaching and learning, achievements, attitudes and well-being of every young person matter [...] This does not mean treating all pupils in the same way. Rather it involves taking account of pupils' varied life experiences and needs. [...] They identify any pupils who may be missing out, difficult to engage, or feeling in some way to be apart from what the school seeks to provide.

In the same report the following groups of students are identified in relation to inclusion: girls and boys; minority ethnic and faith groups, Travellers, asylum seekers and refugees; pupils who need support to learn English as an additional language (EAL); pupils with special educational needs; gifted and talented pupils; children 'looked after' by the local authority; other children, such as sick children, young carers; children from other families under stress; pregnant schoolgirls and teenage mothers; and any pupils who are at risk of disaffection and exclusion. This list 'fragments' the notion of young people into numerous groups and, consequently, inclusion becomes a process of 'managing' many different individuals and groups who are perceived as 'problems'.

It is clearly not sufficient to select a 'good' definition of inclusion (that is, a definition that one agrees with) and ignore all others. Simply selecting a definition does not confine either the theorization or practice of inclusive education to that definition; nor does it eliminate the complexities and contradictions that characterize much of the thinking about what is meant by 'inclusion'. Definitions focusing on different levels of policy and practice are commonly found. As we have seen, much of the commentary on inclusion is concerned with the identification and advocacy of 'good' classroom practice. Yet, inclusion may also be seen either as an education reform programme that ultimately aims at the restructuring of educational systems or as a policy/practice issue within the current structures of education systems. These different considerations are frequently absent from discussions of inclusion, yet we would argue that even in positioning a discussion about inclusion there are necessary interconnections to be considered that require critical engagement with a broader range of issues about the social and economic purposes of education and the nature and meaning of citizenship.

Summing up the above points, we can argue that different understandings of inclusion generate different possible answers to the three parts of the question: *'inclusion for whom, into what and for what purpose?'* In turn, depending on the answer to this question different conceptions of 'inclusion' and 'inclusive education' are generated.

 Case study

Different responses to the question *inclusion for whom, into what and for what purpose?*

First response: Inclusion is about all students with disabilities participating in all aspects of the school life within the regular school to provide them access to the same educational experiences with other students and full citizenship in an inclusive society.

Second response: Inclusion refers to students with disabilities and special education needs and their increased participation within the education system with the aim to provide an education that responds to their individual needs and to prepare them for life after school.

Third response: Inclusion refers to all students actively participating in schools that are organized in such ways that all students are valued and which constantly problematize notions of inclusion and exclusion and of different ways of being.

Looking at these three definitions it becomes evident that they propose different pathways for how inclusion can be achieved. Although the first two definitions are 'narrow' in terms of the group of students they refer to, their implications for an educational system and its functioning are substantially different. The first definition proposes an inclusion project that requires fundamental changes to the educational system in terms of values, attitudes, structure and organization, curriculum arrangements, criteria of achievement, and so on. Implicit in such a definition may be the assumption that schools (and education systems) that are inclusive in this way would respond not only to disabled students but also to other groups of students who experience exclusion and therefore the inclusion of disabled students is part of a more general programme of education reform.

The second definition is also 'narrow' in terms of referring to specific groups of students and it presents an inclusion project that does not require a radical restructuring of existing provisions, policy and practices. Similar definitions of inclusion can be found in many education policy

(Continued)

(Continued)

documents. In addition, in research on teachers' attitudes to inclusion this type of definition is commonly presented as the one teachers tend to agree with. Many writers in the area of inclusive education are critical of this type of definition, which they see as defining integration as inclusion.

The third definition of inclusion is 'broad' and refers to all students. It presents inclusion as an open-ended project where difference is central to negotiating and constructing individual identities. Inclusion and exclusion are not seen as static, but rather in constant interaction. This understanding of inclusion does not present a finite point for the project of inclusion but any outcome will be the result of significant changes in schools.

Realizing inclusion

Depending on the answer to the question *'inclusion for whom, into what and for what purpose*?', a different answer is given also to the questions *'how can inclusion be achieved?'* and *'what constitutes inclusive practice?'* The *realization of inclusion* constitutes the third complexity that we are going to discuss. In the discussion that follows we consider the outcomes of the inclusive project from five different perspectives on the meaning of inclusion.

From a perspective on inclusion that understands it in terms of a continuum of provision there may remain acceptance of placements in special schools, special units and special classes, on the basis of balancing different rights. Thus, the right of participation is given to some groups with the proviso that the rights of other groups (and especially of the 'majority') are not affected. As Smith (1998: 164) argues, 'some of the rhetoric associated with inclusion concerning "rights of the individual" has been construed by some professionals as "incompatible with the common good"'. This 'common good' is safeguarded by 'clauses of conditionality' (Slee, 1996) to the right of participation when the 'appropriateness' of participation is contested. The limitations on participation frame special education (special school, unit or class) as a mechanism for advancing the goal of inclusion. The transition to inclusion is guided by the balancing of rights and therefore those who have been excluded from the mainstream earning the right to return in so far as they cause no harm to the rights of the majority within the mainstream.

An organizational approach to schooling sees schools as organizations that have the potential to instigate and implement change in becoming more inclusive. In this approach inclusion is seen as a process. For example Black-Hawkins et al. (2007: 8) argue that 'inclusion in education is both the means for, and a consequence of, school systems attempting to address issues of inequality by widening access and participation'. They conceptualize inclusive schools as those that both serve a diverse student population and constantly seek to improve the achievements of all their students. However, some of the discussion of the arrangements described in the case studies they present, for example the participation in the school life of students attending the separate 'resourced provision' for students designated as having profound and multiple learning difficulties in one school, have close similarities with what the *Warnock Report* (DES, 1978) referred to as 'locational' integration; there remains a physical separation between the mainstream and special unit even though they are located on the same site.

The work of Ainscow, Booth and Dyson has been very influential internationally through the implementation in schools in many countries of the *Index for Inclusion* (Ainscow et al., 2006). They take a 'principled approach' to education through the articulation of a number of inclusive values including 'equity', 'participation', 'community', 'compassion', 'respect for diversity', 'sustainability' and 'entitlement'. Yet, they argue that the barriers that inhibit participation and learning and which prevent the allocation of resources to support that participation and learning can only be meaningfully specified and overcome within a particular school. According to their approach, an inclusive school is one that is prepared to engage with change rather than one that has reached a perfect state. For writers working with what we can call a 'pragmatic' framework for the realization of inclusion, the balancing of what is 'achievable' at a given time in a given setting with what is ultimately 'desirable' is a constant issue of consideration.

Other approaches to inclusion emphasise inclusion as a political struggle. Leo and Barton (2006) argue that commitment to inclusion is difficult to sustain in the current policy context and that for schools within the most disadvantaged communities, where 'special needs' are most frequently found, the challenges are even greater. Their discussion emphasizes the limits of school leadership and school development for achieving inclusive practice within the structural constraints in which schools operate. In particular, they refrain from presenting a model for schools to follow, but rather highlight the principles of inclusive leadership proposing that central to leadership for inclusion is 'moral leadership' which acknowledges the 'moral values of social inclusion'.

Finally, Allan (2008) uses concepts developed by the philosophers of difference to examine the idea of inclusion, an idea she perceives as political. In particular she uses the concepts of 'subverting', 'subtracting' and 'inventing' to explore possible ways of action for those engaging in inclusion and thus inclusion becomes reframed as a struggle for participation rather than something that is done to young people. Thus, the idea of inclusion is a continuous struggle, not a fixed outcome. Moreover, in conceptualizing inclusion in this way, teachers can avoid a sense of frustration or guilt over their apparent failures because they too are involved in a continuous and contested process rather than with the implementation of a predetermined goal.

The central similarity of all these examples is that they are working within the constraints of the existing educational systems. However, in most of them, participants in the process of becoming more inclusive need to address issues at different levels of the school system. They need to see how staff and students are organized; resources and support systems are utilized; curriculum is developed, presented and assessed; attitudes of the school communities influence understanding, interactions and opportunities for collaboration; and how change can be initiated and what kind of professional development is needed. All these happen while the school is still undertaking numerous statutory processes concerning the identification and assessment of needs, as well as seeking additional resources to meet a range of diverse needs. Thus the school needs to operate within a framework that for students with special educational needs in many educational systems is orientated towards an individual model of dis/ability and need, and at the same time to transcend this model in the process of becoming inclusive.

Thus, even though some schools may be very effective in 'managing' the above processes and in providing at the same time inclusive experiences to their students, this (a) may have no or limited effect in relation to other schools and their practices, (b) probably has no effect at the system level in terms of further change towards a more inclusive system, and (c) may be a precarious process which may fail to be sustained in the long term. As we discuss in Chapter 8, 'inclusive practice' takes place in many schools and classrooms. However, whether this means that schools are becoming more inclusive is questionable.

Outcomes of inclusion

The above discussion leads us to consider a fourth area of complexity in respect of the meaning of inclusion; namely, that of the *outcomes of inclusion*. Since there is no clear agreement about what inclusion is and how it might be realized, it is also difficult to establish consensus about what the outcomes of inclusion should be. There are two aspects to this, *what are the outcomes of inclusion* and *how can they be demonstrated and measured*? Depending on which definition of inclusion one uses, different outcomes and measures may be seen as relevant.

For example, for definitions that perceive the process of inclusion as an alternative to special education provision, a possible measure may be that inclusion provides better short- and long-term educational and social outcomes to students with special education needs than separate systems of special education provision. One central difficulty with the research in this area is that there are methodological and ethical issues involved creating difficulties for the design of studies that compare the same or similar things. Thus, most of these studies are small scale, with small samples and without 'control' groups. Such studies respond more to the question of whether a particular instance of placement is 'effective' for a particular group of students in a particular educational context, rather than to that of whether a particular approach to educating students is effective. This places significant limitations on the 'evidence base' which might demonstrate whether or not the outcomes of inclusion are successful in educational terms.

For definitions that do not see any connection or continuity between special education provision and inclusion, the above measure may also be inappropriate. It may be better to utilize student measures (for example, engagement with learning, achievement, participation of the student population), teacher measures (for example, attitudes, workload, sense of preparedness) and school-level measures (for example, enrolment practices, staff retention, grouping of students, methods of instructions). Numerous studies taking a case study approach exist that explore how inclusion is defined and implemented in specific educational settings or across educational settings.

It can be argued that the more encompassing the definition of inclusion, the more difficult it is to measure it. In the second definition of inclusion detailed above, which focuses on the increased participation of students with special education needs, outcomes (and relevant measures) of inclusion can be set for this specific group of students. However, in a definition like the third one we have described, which looks at inclusion for all students (and perhaps other members of the school community, including teachers), the 'outcomes of inclusion' cannot be separated from broader educational outcomes in any meaningful way. Moreover, as we have previously indicated, not everything that is called and presented as 'inclusive' may actually be experienced as inclusive, precisely because different understandings of inclusion are employed. It is obviously problematic to use 'evidence' about the effectiveness or not of inclusion drawn from one definition to evaluate the outcomes from a different perspective.

Thomas et al. (1998:5–6) argue that 'If principles cannot be evaluated for their veracity nor ethics for their truth, it is crucial that the consequences of the principled policy decision to provide inclusive education are rigorously monitored'. Without denying that it is essential at many levels to examine the 'effectiveness' of inclusion in its implementation, it is perhaps more crucial to unpack whether and to what extent inclusion challenges the weighting of 'costs' and 'benefits' in terms of individual, group and society 'needs' and 'good'.

Points for reflection

Consider what 'benefits' and 'costs' are involved in the pairs of statements below and how they are weighted against each other:

- Peter's disability is such that he won't benefit from a placement in the regular classroom.
- Maya's disability is such that her inclusion in the regular classroom would have a negative effect on the smooth working of the classroom.

- This school is not ready to accept students with disabilities because the necessary resources are not available.
- This school has an academic orientation and, due to her disability, Karla does not fit the school's student profile.

- Teachers do not possess the necessary knowledge to effectively teach students with disabilities.
- It is not part of the role of general classroom teachers to teach students with disabilities.

- Society is not ready at the moment to accept students with disabilities as equal members.
- Students with disabilities will have an adverse effect to other students' well-being.

- Substantial financial investment is needed before inclusion can be implemented in schools.
- Many students without disabilities need further assistance and additional resources in regular schools and it is not fair to invest all these resources on a small group of students.

Critiques of inclusion

In this final section we turn our attention to critique of the inclusion project in order to outline issues that we believe inclusive education still needs to address if it is to continue to hold claims to being a credible project or goal. Inclusive education has been criticized from different perspectives as being *flawed in its conceptualization*. Such criticisms have come from the advocates of more traditional approaches to special education as well as from within the inclusive education movement itself. Finally, perhaps the most powerful critique has been mounted from within the disability movement from those groups, such as the Deaf, who reject the premise upon which inclusive education has been founded by its advocates in the disability movement.

For a number of writers, special education, as a 'separate' or 'sub-system' component of education is inescapable. Bateman (1995) for example, argues that special education is a direct consequence of the bell-shaped distribution of many human learning characteristics. Mainstream education, Bateman argues, is a system that by its very essence is centred on the average needs and abilities of the school population. Even if it were possible to individualize the delivery of education within the mainstream classroom so that all needs were engaged with, such an approach would remain less than optimally effective in terms of learning outcomes and particularly inappropriate for the students at the extremes, the outliers. On this argument, special education provides a 'safety net' for 'regular education' as well as a specialized service for the disabled child. Accordingly, it follows that inclusive education is a 'folly' that does a disservice not only to students with disabilities, but also to other students, teachers and schools. In addition, in terms of a costs/benefits debate, inclusion is seen as a costly mistake.

A second critique of inclusion questions the possibility of a truly transformative approach to educational change at both the school and systems level. This critique is expressed mainly from a post-structural perspective and focuses on the role of *difference* in the inclusive discourse. Graham and Slee (2008) argue that in the process of pointing to the exclusion of specific groups, attention is focused on the 'markers of difference' and thus difference is in fact created by comparison to an implicit norm. In other words, if we return to the Ofsted (2000) groups that may be considered for inclusion, these groupings not only 'fragment' the inclusion focus but reinforce a conception of them as 'problems' due to their difference – difference from a non-specified but dominant notion of what is considered normal.

To some extent according to this critique 'inclusion' cannot simply be constructed as the opposite of 'exclusion'. Inclusion and exclusion are interrelated processes and their interplay constantly creates new inclusive/exclusive conditions and possibilities. This critique is different from that expressed from a special education perspective. These writers are committed to social change in general education and to some extent this is a critique that comes from within the field of inclusive education. Nevertheless, it questions the 'grand project' of inclusive education as a straightforward one.

Finally, two related critiques of inclusion question *whether inclusion is the right course for all and whether there are limits to inclusion* when defined as all students having the access to the same experiences in the same educational settings. The Deaf community has asserted its preference to schools for the Deaf where students and teachers share a common language and culture. Thus the Deaf community adopts a very different position to the issue of access and participation from that of other groups within the Disability Movement and results in a deep division between Deaf organizations and most other organizations of disabled people over how they perceive 'special education'. For the Deaf community inclusion refers first to inclusion within the Deaf community itself. Secondly, it refers to the inclusion of Deaf people within a world dominated by people with hearing. Whereas the first focuses on an issue of identity, the second focuses on the advocacy for social and political rights within a world which is formed by the experiences and forms of interaction that are often alien to the experiences of the Deaf. Similarly, Shakespeare (2006) questions what may constitute inclusion as part of universal design for people with social impairments such as autism. He argues that the development of facilities purposely designed for people with autism may create spaces and times that provide an environment with limited disruptions and distress. He maintains that these solutions tend to 'sound less like barrier-free provision, and more like the specialised and perhaps even segregated provision of solutions for special needs. Ultimately, some people with autism may prefer self-exclusion to inclusion' (Shakespeare, 2006: 49). The last sentence echoes teachers' concerns raised in many playgrounds and classrooms where students with autism are included, and brings together issues of characteristics of impairments, needs and choice.

At the beginning of this chapter it was argued that the power of inclusion as a critical project lies in its extensive focus. Referring to 'education for *all*' or 'inclusion for *all*' has been and still is a powerful message. However this does not mean that we should refrain from exploring what inclusion may mean for different groups and how the experience and outcomes may differ for different individuals and groups. Indeed, presenting inclusion as being 'for' those who have previously been excluded is to focus on those individuals and groups who have been excluded rather than upon the mainstream processes which have defined normality and by doing so have framed the ideologies and mechanisms of exclusion. The real power of the inclusive education movement perhaps lies in its challenge to the power embedded in systems defining who is to be included and on whose terms.

The claim to education for all is based on the acknowledgement that commonalities as well as differences characterize all learners and that one difference, that of impairment, does not and should not override the broader range of commonalities and differences when thinking about the purpose of educational services. Setting cut-off points and exceptions to this principal weakens the power of the idea of inclusion and justifies old and new forms of segregation. Considering inclusion from different perspectives suggests how specific types of difference have been constructed historically as learning and behaviour problems in education systems, and how segregation, exclusion and the language of 'special education' have been used to manage these problems and to maintain the smooth operation of the overall system. Inclusion has had an impact on educational systems with the introduction of disability anti-discrimination legislation, inclusion policies and an emphasis on how schools respond to 'diversity'. However, in many cases inclusion has been reduced to a change of language rather than a change of practice, and in this context it is questionable whether much of the rhetoric and many of the reforms can really be represented as making progress towards genuinely inclusive approaches to education.

Summary

In this chapter it was argued that the failure of inclusive education to become a central force for education reform is not simply a repeat of history. The weakness of the 'inclusive perspective' is characterized by a theoretical vacuum; the great expectations of the early 1990s have been replaced by a lack of critical engagement with the realities of education and schools. This theoretical vacuum is ether hidden in the escapism of much of the post-modern writing on inclusion or the pragmatic watering-down of the under-lying idealism of inclusion. Inclusion as a 'grand project' has *limitations* in terms of its engagement with difference and its partial success in proposing a feasible project for inclusion that can gain consensus and support from students and their families, teachers and schools. Nevertheless, it is by going back to the 'big picture of inclusion' and reformulating it in the light of knowledge, experiences and learning accumulated during the past 20 or so years that we can find a way forward.

Discussion questions

- Can we really refer to inclusion as a singular concept?
- Why is it important to clarify the definition of inclusion?
- Has inclusion turned into a 'soft' approach to dealing with populations that are increasingly perceived in terms of problems to be managed?
- Is this conception of inclusion another way of reinforcing the dominance of normality?
- What are the implications for the future of inclusion?

Further reading

Ainscow, M., Booth, T. and Dyson, A. (2006) *Improving Schools, Developing Inclusion*. London: Routledge.

Allan, J. (2008) *Rethinking Inclusive Education: The Philosophers of Difference in Practice*. Dordrecht: Springer.

Thomas, G. and Loxley, A. (2001) *Deconstructing Special Education and Constructing Inclusion*. Buckingham: Open University Press.

Tomlinson, S. (1982) *A Sociology of Special Education*. London: Routledge and Kegan Paul.

Section 2

Policy Case Studies

In Section 2 we develop the arguments of Section 1 through detailed discussions of policy development. These examine the internationalization of inclusive education, particularly through the activities of intergovernmental agencies and the impact of globalization on education systems in the developing world. We also look at the role of social inclusion within the expanding European Union and its influences on policies of inclusive education.

4

Globalization: Internationalization of Inclusive Education

Chapter overview

In this globalized world, Education for All (EFA) can be seen as an ideal which sets a goal and provides hope and an impetus for transformation. While the 192 member countries of the United Nations verbally express commitment to the concept of Education for All as a worthwhile and noble endeavour, does inclusion mean the same thing to all countries? The EFA framework for action often stalls at the point of implementation but as the Final Report of the Mid-decade Meeting on Education for All in Amman (UNESCO, 1996b) recognized, one of the continuing challenges facing EFA is the fact that there are over 100 million children without access to education and there is an urgent need to respond appropriately in a manner that promotes quality education for all children, including the poor, those in remote locations and those with special educational needs. This chapter is concerned with ideas of 'Education for All' and 'Inclusion' and the ways in which diversity and special education policies and practices are related to these.

Prior to 1980, terms such as 'education for all', 'diversity' and 'inclusion' did not form part of the special education language and engagement. Since then these and other terms such as 'citizenship', 'equal opportunity' 'quality education' and 'social justice' which were not part of the education landscape have entered the vocabulary as academics, policy-makers and practitioners engage with the changing world of special education. In this chapter we explore the development of thinking about inclusive education within the context of universal declarations of support for the principles of 'Education for

All' and 'Cultural Diversity'. In particular, we consider the relationship between the inclusive rhetoric of these universal declarations and commitments and the practical considerations faced by governments, non-governmental organizations (NGOs) and education professions in trying to achieve international targets set for inclusion by the various United Nations agencies. Whether or not these targets are realistic and achievable for developing countries like those in the Caribbean and South America, Asia and Africa and the policy implications of the commitments that have been given towards achieving these goals, are questions of importance. Finally, we consider the broader context within which these questions are currently being addressed.

We have argued (Chapter 3) that the term 'inclusion' means different things to different people. Moreover, the way in which 'inclusion' is conceptualized may differ significantly in the practice of policy-makers, administrators, principals and teachers, and other professionals working in different national educational contexts. The concept of 'inclusion' was developed as a bridge between the less than perfect systems that underpinned special education and what was envisioned to be a new system that would provide the hope for the future. So, the radicalization which underpinned a lot of the thinking about inclusive education was a radicalization which arose from emancipatory ideals in relation to the contribution of education in promoting change in the world. This represented a significant move away from previous charitable and technical ideas about the role of special education.

International perspectives: setting the agenda for inclusion

The international development targets for education set out in the *UN Standard Rules on the Equalization of Opportunities for Persons with Disabilities* (United Nations, 1993: Rule 6) state that: 'States should recognize the principle of equal primary, secondary and tertiary educational opportunities for children, youth and adults with disabilities, in integrated settings. They should ensure that the education of persons with disabilities is an integral part of the educational system.' In its framework for action, emphasis is placed on the importance of a correspondence between basic education and the actual needs, interests, and problems of the participants in the learning process.

The UNESCO *Salamanca Statement* (1994: 11), recognizing the uniqueness of each child and their fundamental human right to education, declared that '(i)nclusion and participation are essential to human dignity and to the exercise and enjoyment of human rights'. The statement is supported by a Framework for Action which strongly supports schools having a child-centred pedagogy supporting all children. This framework suggests that education systems must become inclusive by catering for diversity and special needs, thus creating opportunities for genuine equalization of opportunity. It begins from the premise that differences are a normal part of life and therefore learning should be adapted to cater to those differences, rather than trying to insist that children fit into a perceived 'norm'. As such, governments have been asked to improve their education systems as a priority by adopting laws and policies which support the principles of inclusivity. The *Salamanca Statement* (UNESCO, 1994: ix) advocates:

> Regular schools with this inclusive orientation are the most effective means of combating discriminatory attitudes, creating welcoming communities, building an inclusive society and achieving education for all; moreover, they provide an effective education to the majority of children and improve the efficiency and ultimately the cost effectiveness of the entire education system.

Over the past 20 years, debates about education for children with special needs have become contentious as concern has mounted about the exclusionary role that systems of special education are perceived to have played, particularly in the developed countries of Europe and North America. Critics have argued that one of the underpinning assumptions of 'special educational' policies and practices is that some persons are 'normal' while others, because of medical, neurological, sensory or physical deficits, are not. The result of this conceptualization of need is that significant numbers of children and young people all over the world have been marginalized, denied access to educational opportunities and discriminated against in later life. As Booth (1995: 99) has argued, the term, 'special needs' 'assumes that a division needs to be drawn between "normal" and "less than normal" learners [thus implying] exclusion'. This has led many critics of separate 'special' educational provision, including many disabled people, to argue that the notion of special needs has to be challenged as a 'human rights' issue, rather than being understood as a technical issue about compensatory or remedial education.

Education for All

In 1990, the World Conference on Education for All, which was held in Jomtien, Thailand, made a huge effort to ensure that mass schooling was the global primary agenda for education systems and policy-makers around the world. By the late 1990s, led by United Nations Educational, Scientific and Cultural Organization (UNESCO), the World Bank, the United Nations Development Programme (UNDP), United Nations, the United Nations Population Fund (UNFPA) and the United Nations Children's Fund (UNICEF), national education assessments were undertaken by 183 countries. What has been described as the biggest review of education in history culminated in April 2000, at the World Education Forum in Dakar, Senegal, with countries of the world adopting a *World Declaration on Education* for All (EFA). To many, this was a triumphant symbol of the century-long movement to change the nature and characteristics of existing national educational systems from catering mostly for the elite and middle classes to the largest most comprehensive mass education system ever. This principle was translated at the national level into policies geared to introducing basic education for the masses.

Though Education for All can be seen as an ideal, it sets a goal, something to work toward as a worthwhile endeavour. It provides hope and an impetus for transformation. It is also necessary for national systems of education to have access to the resources and capacity which will enable them to expand and improve comprehensive early childhood programmes; equal educational opportunities for both sexes; improvements in the quality of education for all children; and, the monitoring, implementation and evaluation of national plans. It could be argued that it is very easy for member countries of the United Nations to verbally express commitment to the concept of Education for All as a worthwhile and noble endeavour. Yet it is altogether another matter for the ideal of Education for All to be transformed into a realistic and achievable goal for countries, many of whom are locked into a spiral of indebtedness to international lending agencies.

The Final Report of the Mid-decade Meeting on Education for All in Amman (UNESCO, 1996b: 11) states that:

> The right to education has been powerfully reaffirmed by the near-universal ratification of the United Nations Convention on the Rights of the Child. Yet, there are still over 100 million children without access to education. We must respond urgently with new approaches and strategies capable of bringing quality education within the reach of all, including the poor, the remote and those with special educational needs. This calls for a comprehensive effort tailored to the needs of specific populations and based upon the best available expertise and technology.

It is a difficult to comprehend 100 million children not having any access to education but these children are concentrated in some of the poorest, must politically unstable and socially disadvantaged countries of the world. They predominately live on the continents of Africa, Asia and South America.

Usually when the word 'all' is used, it means 'everyone', so it is interesting that the report states that there is an urgent need to respond in a manner that promotes quality for all children and then qualifies the term 'all' by stating 'including the poor, those in remote locations, and those with special educational needs', because 'all' should have covered each and every one. 'All' cannot mean some and not others.

These conflicting messages are made by very powerful organizations that shape and drive the way we think about inclusive education, diversity and inclusive practices. Usually, when teachers in the underdeveloped or the developing world speak about inclusive education, they mean special education and they usually make references to categories of special educational need. They still talk about doing things under the umbrella of being benevolent; that is, about having a humanitarian or charitable approach to education.

This is a true story told by a Ghanaian lecturer to his undergraduate students in Trinidad in 1990:

> 'My Uncle – he was responsible for my upbringing, and he was blind … so, class, what would you think? Do you think that he was disabled?' Everyone had their new knowledge from all sorts of professional learning short courses, said 'Yes, he was disabled'. This was based on the knowledge that the uncle was legally blind. The lecturer proclaimed 'Well I will tell you that he wasn't' And the class looked at him shocked. They asked him to explain further because clearly there was something wrong with the lecturer's uncle that needed to be fixed. He explained. 'My uncle was not disabled, because to me, he was my uncle, he was a human first.'

That incident teaches us something very profound. As humans, we have to go back to the heart of the subject. We have to begin by acknowledging the personhood of all people. We have to go beyond labels and recognize that under the skin, we are all the same, and there must be some level or some balance where we accommodate all people. And, more importantly, when we say 'all', we do not have to qualify it by saying 'the poor, the disadvantaged, the disabled, and so on'.

Cultural diversity

Following the events of 11 September 2001 when the World Trade Center and the Pentagon in the USA were attacked, the thirty-first session of the UNESCO General Conference adopted the *Universal Declaration on Cultural Diversity*. This was perceived as an opportunity for countries to express their support for intercultural dialogue as part of a roadmap to peace in the world. However, it can be challenging for all peoples from all countries to understand and indeed experience cultural diversity in the same way. Enshrined in 12 articles are ethical considerations which are intended to act as guidelines for supporting member states in developing policy which would be appropriate and culturally meaningful in their societies.

Cultural diversity can refer to *individual characteristics* such as race, gender, age, disability; *social characteristics* such as ethnic background, language, nationality, religion, family structure; and can include *cultural characteristics* such as mode of dress and appearance, modes of artistic expression, and so on. No list of cultural characteristics is comprehensive and each person is imbued with a number of cultural attributes that contribute to their idea of themselves.

Similarly, special education needs are not simply the product of isolated medical factors but are created, exacerbated managed and ignored in the contexts of poverty, war, epidemics. Historically, special education needs have been linked to a lack of understanding about differences between different ethnic groups. UNESCO's *Universal Declaration of Cultural Diversity* (2002a) recognizes the complexities of defining cultural diversity and in Article 1 'Cultural diversity: the common heritage of humanity', it is stated that: 'Culture takes diverse forms across time and space. This diversity is embodied in the uniqueness and plurality of the groups and societies making up humankind. As a source of exchange, innovation and creativity, cultural diversity is as necessary for humankind as biodiversity is for nature' (UNESCO, 2002a: 13).

In any society, cultural differences, social and historical experiences, and political pragmatism and principles are each likely to impact upon both policy and practice of inclusion. Article 2 'From cultural diversity to cultural pluralism', attempts to address these issues. It is concerned with the development of 'policies for the inclusion and participation of all citizens as guarantees of social cohesion, the vitality of civil society and peace' (UNESCO, 2002a: 13).

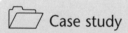 Case study

> Education has been hailed as the great liberator of people. Let us consider the case of the Dalits of India. Though the Dalits have been afforded some measure of education, centuries of entrenchment in a caste system have ensured that this group of people experience ongoing exploitation so that they remain at the bottom of the social and economic barrel. Their jobs have changed from being at the lowest level of the caste-feudal system to being at the lowest level of the new employment structures (Velaskar, 1998). Despite the opening up of some educational opportunities, they continue to be employed in the low-paying, low-skilled jobs. How does this situation sit with the idea that education brings about the emancipation of the masses?

Globalization: concepts and definitions

The term 'globalization' came into use following the crisis experienced in the early 1970s within the capitalist economic system, when many transnational corporations, governments of the industrialized countries, and international financial institutions attempted to restructure the world economy in an effort to restore their decreasing profit levels and ensure the survival of capitalism.

It became a trendy buzzword in the 1980s, and like the term 'inclusion', the more popular the term 'globalization' became, the less there was a shared understanding of what it meant. Globalization began to encapsulate and even replace other fashionable ones like 'internationalization' which is 'the increasing interwovenness of national economies through international trade'; and, 'transnationalization' which is 'the increasing organisation or production on a cross-border basis by multinational organisations' (Hoogvelt, 1997: 114). Globalization has acquired a very broad spectrum of meanings which cover the social, economic and political changes which take place due to this restructuring of the world's economy so that the business sector could discover new ways of maximizing their profits. It should be no surprise that the nature and impact of globalization varies considerably across different countries. The position of different countries in relation to the world economy, the relative geo-political power of nations, together with regional economic and political interrelationships may significantly nuance the development and impact of globalization across different localities.

 Point for reflection

Likewise, terms like inclusion and diversity were adopted within the policy pronouncements of international agencies like the UN and the World Bank to make global statements that were intended to focus attention on the needs of the developing and underdeveloped world. On the other hand, expressions like 'education for all' too often refer to 'basic education' and not necessarily to the forms of education that would be expected to be delivered to the average child in the average classroom in the developed world. Moreover, basic education is relative to context, so basic education in one country would not necessarily equate with basic education in another. Basic in parts of India would be different from basic in other parts of India and certainly different from Asia and the various countries of Africa and the Caribbean and Latin America.

Arjun Appadurai (1993: 28) recognizes the complex nature of globalization and explains that it is:

a complex, overlapping, disjunctive order which cannot any longer be understood in terms of existing centre-periphery models. Nor is it susceptible to simple models of push and pull (re: migration theory), or of surpluses and deficits (re: traditional balance of trade), or of consumers and producers (re: neo-Marxist theories of development).

It is indeed multidimensional. Giddens (1990: 64) defines globalization as: 'the intensification of the world wide social relations which link distant localities in such a way that local happenings are shaped by events occurring many miles away and vice versa'. He recognizes four intersecting levels of globalization which are labelled as: the world capitalist economy; the international division of labour; the world military order and the nation-state system; and, includes a fifth which he refers to as cultural globalization. Brine (1999: 27) likens this to the somewhat older idea of cultural imperialism which 'ensures that post colonized nations remain attached to their colonizers'.

Cultural globalization is most visible through the media: television, video, films, music, advertisements and the like. The media dictates the pace and trends of the global market and constructs the form of youth culture and accentuates US hegemonic influence. Cultural globalization in its many forms seems to be linked to neo-colonialism as well as US imperialism, which is perceived as an attempt to claim global supremacy and Americanize the world. Here, the old forms of disparity are compounded by the transnational corporations in a highly complex form, and, result in promoting the traditional inequalities of race, ethnicity, gender and class.

If we look at the latest indicator of globalization, the global financial crisis (GFC), every week stories emerge about more job losses, more losses incurred by manufacturing companies and financial institutions, more unscrupulous investors who are no longer able to hide their mythical success as a result of the economic downturn and more share market fluctuations and the negative growth of major economies of the world like Iceland, Korea, Singapore, the USA and the UK. We also read about multi-billion dollar bailout packages for floundering economies with banks, mortgage companies and various industries making the case that these are necessary to ensure that the various country economies survive. What, then, about education for all, inclusion, diversity, gender and equality of opportunities?

 Point for reflection

Some facts from UNESCO:

In 2005, 1.4 billion people lived on US$1.25 or less a day.
10 million die every year of hunger and hunger-related diseases.
Rising food prices may push 100 million people deeper into poverty.
Statistics show that fewer children below five are undernourished – from 33 per cent in 1990 to 26 per cent in 2006.

What if multi-billion dollar bail-outs for failing financial companies could extend to poverty and education for all in the most comprehensive manner?

What sort of inclusive education would be required for the hundreds of maimed children of the Gaza strip or the child soldiers of Africa or street children of Latin and South America or the gypsies of Eastern Europe?

These are all people who sit at the margins of society. Poverty and oppression do terrible things to people and when desperation sets in, there are usually violent consequences. It is all very well that we could sit in our middle-class states and proclaim that violence and theft do not solve problems, but people who sit on the other side of the fence experience the world differently from us.

When we consider the current world scenario, do we feel empowered to do anything constructive about inclusive education in the world? What are some of the practical strategies that we could employ?

Is EFA achievable?

The 2008 *Global Monitoring Report* (UNESCO, 2007) has drawn attention to some positive and inspiring national and regional performances. For example Tanzania and Ethiopia have both reduced the number of children out of school by over 3 million. In a region marked by deep gender inequalities, Bangladesh now has as many girls as boys reaching secondary school. In Latin America, several countries are enrolling and keeping more children in schools through innovative cash transfer programmes for the poorest households, with payments made conditional on school attendance and health visits. Most remarkably, Mexico's Oportunidades programme, one of the country's largest education schemes, is now being pilot tested in the New York City school system.

On the challenging side, the report also states that an estimated 75 million children of primary school age worldwide are currently out of school (which certainly compares favourably with the 1996 estimate of 100 million highlighted in the *Mid-Decade Meeting on Education for All*, referred to earlier in this chapter. Current projections put forward in the 2008 *Global Monitoring Report* suggest that at least 29 million children will still be missing out on their right to an education in 2015, but this is no doubt an encouraging trend. Yet any optimism should be tempered by recognition that a further 776 million adults, or 16 per cent of the world's population, lack even basic literacy skills. Two-thirds of these are women.

It is very easy for member countries of the United Nations to verbally express commitment to the concept of Education for All as a meaningful and note-worthy undertaking. It is altogether another matter as to whether Education for All is a realistic and achievable goal for countries that are already locked into a spiral of indebtedness to international lending agencies and where there are large balance of payments deficits. Action plans need to be a part of a national plan for sustainable development and should be backed by finan-cial resources linked to sustainable sources of income. Unfortunately, for developing countries, this can very often be more of a dream than a reality when, for instance, as many as one in three children are living in poverty in Latin America and the Caribbean (Williams, 2001).

According to UNESCO (2001) achieving Education for All 'will require sus-tained, intensive and co-ordinated action on several fronts. Transforming resource inputs into learning outcomes requires not just financial investment but also effective education systems, the right mix of resources (for example, teachers and learning materials) and an overall national context of sound eco-nomic and social policies'. There is a need for a comprehensive, integrated, long-term, collective approach to education within the context of national, sub-regional, regional and global imperatives. There is a need to recognize that standards differ across the world and the support services that are required should match the needs. Too often strategies and interventions are determined by external bodies rather than through locally developed strategies which sup-port self-determination. It is very difficult to implement full support for inclu-sive education when the basic infrastructure that is needed to support education is not there. What is to be done in countries like Indonesia, Vietnam and Laos where it is common to find two teachers supporting six classes, and classrooms that are uncomfortable, dirty and without floors and ceilings? What does inclusive education mean in these sorts of schools?

To a large extent problems related to the implementation of Education for All are related to economic disparity between countries; cultural imperial-ism which often means that countries of the North dictate the pace and direction to countries of the South. A lack of political will at a global level to do what is right in terms of equitable distribution of resources together with a lack of political will at country levels continue to be major obstacles to change and educational development. In addition teachers in these countries are commonly paid such low salaries that they are often forced to have two or three jobs in order to fulfil their obligations and take care of their families. They are faced with inadequate school resources and infrastructure, and are requested to implement projects in systems that are ill-equipped to deliver efficiencies. Similarly, governments in developing countries, rather than being supported to streamline their outdated internal systems which have mostly been inherited from former colonial models, are granted international loans which focus on externally prioritized goals with aid often linked to the purchase of expertise and resources from developed countries, thus contributing further to a cycle of entrapment in inefficiencies.

Summary

This chapter has demonstrated that designing and implementing an EFA system in a country is not as simple as plugging in a computer and loading the software. Though it may be an international goal and touted as a national priority, EFA has to be considered and understood in terms of the historical, social, cultural, financial and political contexts within each specific country. While offering what seems to be an opportunity for real educational engagement with the poorest and most disenfranchised groups within society, there are a series of challenges that need to be overcome. These need to be worked through in an honest manner, recognizing the realities of the situation, and developing a series of strategies which will support the total development of a country's education system in a manner that is respectful and uplifting to all. If, as educators, we require our students to become critically active citizens of the world, then we need to recognize the relationship between power and knowledge, and to acknowledge that power lies in the guises of race, gender, class, and labels of abilities and disabilities. This is not going to disappear unless we learn to unpack and deconstruct these labels and the attendant practices which support their perpetuation in a negative manner.

Discussion questions

- Are inclusive practices really inclusive?
- Is there a tension between the ideal of inclusion and the eventual implementation of 'inclusive' practices in a globalized world?
- Has inclusion become an instrument for managing and accommodating difference?
- Has the concept of Education for All become a mechanism which seeks to prepare the underdeveloped world and the poor to rise to the low-skilled jobs of the modern occupational ladder, that is, new order of 'hewers of wood and drawers of water'?
- What are the consequences of differential access to the resources and capacity for the expansion and improvement of the quality of education?

Further reading 📖

UNESCO (1990) 'Background document: World Conference on Education for All – meeting basic learning needs'. Available at http://unesdoc.unesco.org/images/0009/000975/097552e.pdf (accessed 30 October 2008).

UNESCO (1994) *The Salamanca Statement and Framework for Action on Special Needs Education.* Available at www.unesco.org/education/pdf/SALAMA_E.PDF (accessed 30 October 2008).

UNESCO (2002) *Universal Declaration on Cultural Diversity.* Paris: UNESCO. Available at http://unesdoc.unesco.org/images/0012/001271/127160m.pdf (accessed 30 October 2008).

UNESCO (2008) Special issue. *The UNESCO Courier.*

UNESCO (2006) *EFA Glopal Monitoring Report 2007. Strong foundations: Early childhood care and education.* Paris: UNESCO. Available from www.unesco.org/en/efareport/reports/2007-early-childhood/

UNESCO (2007) *EFA Global Monitoring Report 2008. Education for All by 2015: Will we make it?* Paris: UNESCO. Available from: http://www.unesco.org/en/efareport/reports/2008-mid-term-review/

Velaskar, P. (1998) 'Ideology, education and the political struggle for liberation: change and challenge among the Dalits of Maharashtra', in S. Shukla and R. Kaul (eds), *Education, Development and Underdevelopment.* New Delhi: Sage Publications.

5

The Impact of International Agencies on Inclusive Policies

Chapter overview

Economic world classifications have identified that of the 194 countries in the world, 23 have high-income status and are the main stakeholders in economic agencies such as the International Monetary Fund (IMF), the International Bank for Reconstruction and Development (IBRD) and the Inter-American Development Bank (IADB). These agencies largely determine the rules that frame the development and implementation of social and educational policy for the rest of the world. While the policies of these agencies claim to be firmly committed to the goal of poverty alleviation, others have argued that their policies have led to the economic ruin of many developing countries through macro-stabilization and structural adjustment programmes. Critics have argued that one of the underpinning assumptions of 'special educational' policies and practices is that some persons are 'normal' while others, because of medical, neurological, sensory or physical deficits, are not. The result of this conceptualization of need is that significant numbers of children and young people all over the world have been marginalized, denied access to educational opportunities and discriminated against in later life. This chapter will use case studies to explore international systems promoted by agencies such as UNESCO and the IBRD and their impact upon inclusive education in local contexts.

Policies of international funding agencies

International organizations play a central role in educational policy-making both at the international and national level. Some, such as the Organisation for Economic Co-operation and Development (OECD) and UNESCO, exert influence through research and policy development at the intergovernmental level. Others, like the World Bank and the IMF, exert their influence through borrowing for major development and reconstruction projects. The World Bank is the largest external funder of education in the world and is therefore able to assert considerable influence over the delivery of education in the countries where loans are granted. When the World Bank accepted education as an area of focus, its primary motivation according to Jones and Coleman (2005: 39) 'was to protect its own investments in physical infrastructure'. As the name implies, the World Bank is a bank. Unlike other intergovernmental organizations (IGOs) and bilateral government donors who provide aid for educational development through grants, the World Bank provides loans and credits. As with any other banking system, when money is borrowed, it must be paid back with interest. This differs significantly from the grants provided by IGOs and government donors for which payment agreements are not strictly enforced.

The International Bank for Reconstruction and Development (also known as the World Bank) was formed after the Second World War to provide capital support for reconstruction and development projects. Initially neither education nor social policy programmes were items on its agenda. Subsequently, in the late 1950s, there was a shift in the original focus of the bank from reconstruction to lending mainly to poorer newly independent, developing countries (Kapur et al., 1997). By the 1970s, the bank had formed an Education Department employing a small group of education professionals whose interests primarily lay in equity and the education of marginalized groups, including the poor. As a result of their work, the bank's funding in primary education grew from 4.2 per cent of overall bank education sector lending between 1963 and 1968 to 22.9 per cent between 1975 and 1979 (Jones, 1992). While UNESCO was proclaiming to governments around the world the importance of universal primary schooling, the bank's position was that minimum basic education would only become possible when resources were available. In the 1970s, lending focused around capital improvements like school construction, technical vocational projects and higher education. By the 1980s, the bank's *World Development Report* indicated that the solution to alleviating poverty lay in the investment in human capital, and this marked a renewed focus by the bank on investment in education.

In the 1980s, the bank, working in tandem with its sister organization the IMF, spearheaded a series of macroeconomic structural adjustment policies where loans to help developing countries whose economies were 'reeling' from the cost of oil and the diminished importance of their agricultural production were tied to conditions related to the adoption of IMF macro-stabilization policies. These policies frequently included depreciation of national currencies, maintenance of low inflation and balance of payments equilibrium, and the opening of local markets to foreign trade and investment. Throughout the 1970s and 1980s many developing countries borrowed more than they could afford to repay and compounded the problem by investing badly. Yet such borrowing was encouraged by Western governments. Some recipient governments were corrupt and transferred considerable sums of money from loans into private offshore bank accounts. Moreover, the economies of these countries were not growing fast enough to repay their loans so that they fell behind in their repayments, becoming trapped in a vicious circle of debt.

Michel Chossudovsky (1994), Professor of Economics at the University of Ottawa, in his web-based article on 'Global impoverishment and the IMF-World Bank economic medicine' points out that although both the World Bank and the IMF claim to be firmly committed to the goal of poverty alleviation, their policies have led to the economic ruin of many developing countries. The macro-stabilization and structural adjustment programmes which were conditions set by these agencies for the renegotiation of their external debts were often in practice not in keeping with the Bretton Woods agreement, which was based on the principle of supporting economic reconstruction and the stabilizing of the major exchange rates. Countries who dared to resist these (de)stabilizing practices were 'black-listed' resulting in further economic hardship and isolation. For many developing countries facing this situation, it was difficult to know which way to turn. The tightening screw of economic adjustment was reinforced by the political interventionism of the USA in particular in the affairs of developing countries. The *Truman Doctrine* of March 1947 gave the USA the right to intervene in the affairs of other countries in order to protect 'free peoples from communist subversion'. McMichael (1995: 39) has gone so far as to argue that in combining the forces of General Agreement on Tariffs and Trade (GATT), the World Bank and North American Free Trade Association, the USA has coerced other nation states to submit to the rules and culture of the global market on a world scale.

More recently, non-governmental lobbyists, the UN and even some World Bank insiders began applying pressure on the bank to modify its approach to economic engagement and consider strategies to support debt relief, provide greater support for the poorer countries by allowing them to have a say in the bank's governance and move away from the focus of structural adjustment loans and conditions. Over time the bank's policies have moved from being highly prescriptive to being more conciliatory in their approach. A significant landmark occurred in 2000 when an alliance of 120 US NGOs were successful in lobbying the US Congress for legislation to be passed requiring the US Executive Directors at the IMF, World Bank and other multilateral development banks to end abusive structural adjustment practices and refrain from imposing user fees upon poor countries for education and primary health care (*Bloomberg News*, 2000).

Point for reflection

Understandably, governments from developing countries make every attempt to apply for funding for their development initiatives. Often attached to these loans are conditions that ensure that the developing countries remain firmly in debt with little left to spend on the essential services of health and education. From a public relations perspective, the idea of a lump sum loan sounds like a lot of money and it provides a very impressive headline for the media. However, when the money is allocated and the average apportionment per child is calculated, the provision may be as little as US$2 per child.

What does that say about education for all?
What does that say about inclusive education?
What are some of the tensions between the ideal of inclusion and the eventual implementation of inclusive practices in a globalized world?

According to Carr-Hill (2004: 331) almost one-third of the world's population live in countries where the goals of Education for All 'remain a dream rather than a realistic proposition'. A 2002 UNESCO report suggests that US$5.6. billion, which is more than double the World Bank's estimate, would be required per year to implement EFA (UNESCO, 2002b). Yet, the total amount required for this task is less than the amount quoted for the most recent Iraq war which started in 2003. Projected aid flows do not live up to expectations and promises and this trend continues in 2008/09 with the global financial crisis in full swing.

One can question the subtext of EFA. The world's most powerful economies and agencies (that is, the West or the North) seem driven to 'fix' the world according to their own likeness, standards and concepts. Carr-Hill believes that EFA as a (Western) project has not been adequately problematized. Amartya Sen (2003) in his speech to the Commonwealth education conference in Edinburgh recognized that:

> Basic education is not just an arrangement for training to develop skills (important as that is), it is also a recognition of the nature of the world, with its diversity and richness, and an appreciation of the importance of freedom and reasoning as well as friendship. The need for that understanding – that vision – has never been stronger.

Sen argued that it is important to close the education gaps and remove the enormous disparities in educational access and achievement. If we do not, not only are the poor and the disadvantaged treated unjustly but the world is also a less secure place for us all.

Intergovernmental agencies also influence national education policy in a variety of ways. They create 'soft' spaces by virtue of their global multilateral nature where 'soft' laws can be shaped, fashioned, discussed, ratified and enforced to the extent that it could be in a global context. According to Abbot and Snidal (2000), 'soft' law can be juxtaposed to 'hard' law. International law can be described as 'hard' when the three criteria of obligation, precision and delegation are strong. It becomes 'soft' when one or two of the criteria are absent, not enforced, or only partially so. However it must be understood that these laws are acted out to varying degrees along a continuum.

 Case study

The United Nations *Declaration of Human Rights* (1948) is well known for its pronouncement that everyone has a right to free education at least in the elementary or fundamental stages. The declaration was conceived as a statement of objectives which would be a guide to governments and agencies to promote the cause of equity and social justice in education. However, in terms of obligation, precision and delegation, it is weak and unenforceable though it is legally binding. It is indeed a contradiction.

The document then is used as the gold standard for basic human rights and education in the world. All other laws on human rights and education always refer to this one. Its importance lies in its usefulness for encouraging states to adhere to its standards. There is no overt force. Rather, there is an understanding and an expectation of what is to be achieved. It is about belonging to an elite club and valuing that membership by adhering to its rules even if it is with some exceptions.

Consider how soft law may be used to direct the course of education at international, national, regional, local levels in both the North and the South?

By radicalizing the concepts of space and time, globalization has effectively reordered the world into new regional blocs. The emergence of the European Union in an effort to re-create the countries of Europe is one such example. National boundaries are no longer applicable in the ways that they once were because to some extent at least they have been overtaken by effects of technological change, financial interdependency and the growth of world culture. The outcome of this interdependency, however, has not resulted in an evening out of development across countries. Quite the opposite has been the case as the interpenetration of markets through free-market globalization has created new, and reinforced old, economic disparities across the world.

One of the important considerations in terms of the recent resurgence of the ideals of universal education is that while this movement has made considerable contributions to the improvement of educational opportunities and facilities for children in some countries, in many countries the scale of the intervention has been far from inclusive of all children. Policies and provision of educational support for children with special educational needs for example often remain separate from the broader banner of Education for All. The progress review of EFA at the 2000 World Education Forum in Dakar reported that a key challenge was 'to ensure that the broad vision of EFA as an inclusive concept is reflected in national government and funding agency policies' (UNESCO, 2000: para. 19). On the other hand, Mundy (2007: 2) argues that there are two main reasons why the global promise of EFA has moved beyond international rhetoric. First, there is the emergence of a broad united consensus among the G8 countries of what constitutes international development. Secondly, this promised focus has linked development to democracy, good governance and human rights more so than ever before, while also asserting the primacy of markets and capitalism. The North has therefore dictated the parameters of what it considers as its ideal and since education is perceived as an honourable social intervention, it adequately straddles both interpretations of development. There is also a growing interest in what Mundy (2007: 2) refers to as 'global redistributive justice' in part by the emergence of a new American imperialism, but also in the new social movements against poverty, aids and environmental disaster promoted through celebrity politics.

Local contexts: UNESCO and the World Bank

The world can hardly be described as a stable place. Political unrest, conflict between political groups and governments abound and natural and man-made disasters occur on a regular basis. Because all things are intricately inter-related, pockets of instability easily have consequences well beyond their immediate reach, with the potential to affect the general health, well-being and education of children across the globe, especially those in the developing world or in underprivileged areas of the developed world. The United Nations *Millennium Development Goals Report* (2008) stated that 'the number of refugees worldwide, has increased significantly over the last few years, primarily because of the conflict in Iraq'. Overall, today there are in the region of more than 42 million displaced people. More than 26 million people have been uprooted by violence or persecution but remain within the borders of their own countries. In these situations, girls are particularly at risk as a result of physical danger such as rape, poverty and early marriages.

The Millennium Declaration of September 2000 adopted by 189 nations and signed by 147 heads of state and governments identified eight Millennium Development Goals with associated actions and targets focused upon global development and cohesion. These goals set quantified targets for addressing extreme poverty in respect of income, hunger, disease, lack of adequate shelter, and exclusion while promoting gender equality, education and environmental sustainability.

The goals sound magisterial and impressive but 'the road to hell is paved with good intentions' and there are several inherent problems with the approach. While the developing countries (who need the most support) are responsible for the achievement of the first seven goals, which include eradication of poverty, achieving universal primary education and gender equality, the achievement of these goals require partnership with the developed nations and international development agencies. Yet, despite targets being established for the amount of aid to be distributed, there are no binding commitments imposed upon the developed countries nor are the UN agencies given the authority to support the various endeavours of the developing countries. Instead, the emphasis is placed on international fund-raising activities, the involvement of high-profile rock stars and appeals to the political leaders of the developed world.

As we move beyond the mid-point of the Millennium Development Goals the world is faced with new crises, including in particular a serious economic downturn, increasing concerns over climate change, shortages of food and energy sources, and financial mayhem. The likelihood of these Millennium Development Goals being achieved within the designated time frame looks to be remote.

Emerging issues

Official development assistance (ODA) is the term that is used to refer to contributions from donor government agencies, multilateral institutions, bilateral donors and middle-income developing countries to finance the economic development and financing of least developing countries (LDCs). The world has changed considerably over the past two decades. Countries that were once described as developing have now risen to the category/ranks of middle-income economies and are now themselves contributing to the economic and political economies of the South. Also the uses of ODA have changed within the past decade where middle-income economies use ODA to acquire specific forms of support. For example, they may use the resources to acquire specific technical expertise and perhaps attract specific kinds of capital flows from private investors. Least developing countries use ODA to support infrastructure and basic health and education services.

One of the emerging challenges is that there are now in excess of 1,000 donor agencies, including 56 bilateral and 230 multilateral institutions, and there is concern that they are not working in harmony, with different initiatives contradicting or duplicating each other in terms of approach and focus. This poses added burdens on the countries who are receiving the aid and often results in confusion within the various agencies on the ground where the need is greatest. The UN Non-Governmental Liaison Service (2008) reports that in 2005, there were approximately 65,000 worldwide donor activities – 20,000 more than in 1997. There was also an expansion in the number of donor countries with countries who were former recipients becoming donors or on the verge of doing so. In 2007, non-G7 countries contributed US$29 billion and in 2006 ODA from the South totalled US$12.6 billion. While some developing countries like China and Egypt have transitioned into becoming donor countries to the World Bank's International Development Agency, several developing countries have not been able to cope with the emerging crises. It is no doubt encouraging to note that about 29 per cent of concessional or discounted lending now originates from countries in the global South, but this situation is now highly volatile as the economies of the world are slowing down. Emerging economies are faced with sudden drops in commodity prices as larger economies either favour spending to revitalize local labour or on indebtedness based on inaccurate projections.

Issues of gender

The Millennium Development Goals establish a range of global aspirations for the improvement of the lives of women through cross-cutting initiatives that pervade the goals and the declaration. Three of the four new targets added to the Millennium Development Goals in 2007 focus specifically upon women: achievement of full and productive employment and decent work for all, including women and young people; achievement of universal access to reproductive health by 2015; and, achievement of universal access to treatment of HIV/AIDS for all those who need it by 2010.

A serious omission from these goals is any target for the reduction of violence against women. Violence cannot be separated from, and is interwoven into, complex social situations such as poverty, lack of education, gender inequality, maternal ill health, child mortality and HIV/AIDS. When women become central to the planning process as legitimate members of the management and accountability process, then there will be a positive marked effect on ensuring that development aid reaches the poorest levels of societies to provide food, basic education and medication, a reduction in infant and maternal mortality, together with medical support to relieve epidemics like HIV/AIDS malaria and measles. In agrarian societies the support of women is also required for sound environmental management.

Approximately 65 per cent of the children who do not attend school are girls and 66 per cent of the global citizens who are illiterate are women. Research has shown that women with less education are more likely to experience violence in the home. It also shows that secondary education is linked to employment opportunities. However, until a critical mass is achieved in order to challenge the status quo, the pioneering women are still at risk from men who feel threatened by this new way of understanding the shifting balance of power.

 Point for reflection

Consider some of the social situations that may occur in various parts of the world where girls are at risk and face barriers preventing access to education.
Suggest strategies that could be used to support the education of girls in the developing and least developed countries of the world.
Identify ways in which the curriculum could contribute to gender inequality.

Like two sides of a coin, inclusion and exclusion occur simultaneously. It has to be asked whether intergovernmental policies such as those set out in the Millennium Development Goals are really about inclusion or are more about maintaining order and social cohesion, particularly in poor and developing countries. Underdeveloped and developing countries usually have a colonial heritage. Access to funding to support future capacity-building, including enhancement of education systems generally and provision of basic education specifically, are important aspects of those countries' development plans. Yet opportunities for access to this funding is framed by the global relations that in the past have created the very inequalities that developing countries are seeking to free themselves from.

 Point for reflection

If you could develop the perfect education system, what would it look like?
What indicators would you use to track the progress of programmes that deal with poverty, education, gender equality and sustainable development?
What would you do to support education in developing countries and least developed countries?

Ideas like inclusion and basic education for all are not isolated events that could be cured or fixed with a mathematical formula or a few recipes. Issues related to inclusion, diversity and educational access and opportunity cannot realistically be addressed in isolation from the wider issues of poverty, debt relief and health. It is easy for middle-class people in developed countries to speak about choice, but choice only becomes truly possible when conditions are set to support a person's freedom to choose. We would argue that if you are poor you do not have the freedom to choose because your life is controlled by poverty, fear, sickness and the experience of a demoralized state. Poor people simply hope for the best in what often seems to be a hopeless situation or resort to violence as a way of taking control of the situation.

In 2000, almost every country along with every international body and every world leader pledged to achieve the eight key Millennium Development Goals. Then, 2008 marked the mid-point towards the projected achievement of the 2015 Millennium Development Goals. At that point some progress had been made with regard to education. Among other things, there were 41 million more children in school. However, there continued to be enormous challenges. At least 72 million children were not in school and many more were receiving poor quality education. To recognize the enormity of the task ahead, the mid-term report highlighted the facts that there are still 980 million people who live on less than US$1 a day, that half of the developing world lacks basic education, that over 33 million people are living with HIV/AIDS and more than 1 million people die of malaria every year, one child every second. Close to 1 billion people (that is, one-sixth of all people on the planet) do not have enough food to eat. If one had to think about the basic necessities of life, if you are hungry, you cannot engage with education. By contrast, today we hear of billions being given to bail-out failing banks and businesses and other financial systems. Unfortunately, the hungry cannot wait for the economy to turn around.

□ Summary

In this globalized world, Education for All can be seen as an ideal which sets a goal and provides hope and an impetus for transformation. While the 192 member countries of the United Nations verbally express commitment to the concept of Education for All as a worthwhile and noble endeavour, does inclusion mean the same thing to all countries? Is there a tension between the ideal of inclusion and the eventual implementation of inclusive practices in a globalized world? What are the consequences of differential access to the resources and capacity for the expansion and improvement of the quality of education? The EFA framework for action often stalls at the point of implementation but as the Final Report of the Mid-decade Meeting on Education for All in Amman (1996) recognized, one of the continuing challenges facing EFA is the fact that there are over 100 million children without access to education and there is an urgent need to respond appropriately in a manner that promotes quality education for all children, including the poor, those in remote locations and those with special educational needs.

 Discussion questions

- Have the policies of international funding agencies supported the growth of inclusive or exclusive systems of education in developing countries?
- Have the policies promoted indigenous social and economic development or have they merely replicated the value systems of the developed world in ways designed to serve the interests of those developed countries that dominated the international aid and lending systems?

Further reading

Mundy, K. (2007) 'Education for All: paradoxes and prospects of a global promise', in D.P. Baker and A.W. Wiseman (eds), *Education for All: Global Promises, National Challenges*, International Perspectives on Education and Society Series, vol. 8, pp. 1–30.

UNESCO (2007) *EFA Global Monitoring Report 2008. Education for All by 2015: Will We Make It?* Paris: UNESCO. Available from www.unesco.org/en/efareport/reports/2008-mid-term-review/ (accessed on 16 March 2009).

UNESCO (2008) *EFA Global Monitoring Report 2009. Overcoming Inequality: Why Governance Matters.* Paris: UNESCO. Available from www.unesco.org/en/efareport/reports/2009-governance/ (accessed on 16 March 2009).

United Nations (2008) *The Millennium Development Goals Report 2008*. New York: United Nations.

6

The European Union: A Common Policy on Inclusion?

Chapter overview

In an expanding European Union[1] (EU) increasingly concerned with the diversity of the member nation states, issues of social cohesion and social inclusion have become paramount. The European Union social policies are complex and characterized by conflicting and competing forces including neo-liberal economic agendas and different egalitarian constructions and traditions. In fact, inclusion is critical for the survival and success of the European Union as an entity. It is through a process of negotiating inclusion as well as exclusion and their meanings that the European Union can guarantee its existence and achieve its economic, social and political aims. In this chapter we explore two notions of inclusion that can be found in the EU policy. The first concerns the relationship between social inclusion and exclusion in the formation of a cohesive European identity. The second looks at the idea of inclusion in European education policy development. In the first section of the chapter we provide a brief overview of the development of European social policy.[2] This is structured through a historical reading of the European Treaties and the growing prominence of social policy in that process with specific discussion on the European Union disability policy. In the second section we present a content analysis of European Union publications that relate to special education and educational inclusion. While the first section of this chapter focuses on policy development and its drivers, the second is more concerned with policy implementation. The conclusion brings the two together by drawing parallels between inclusion at the EU level and in education.

The European Union social policy and disability

Since the *Paris Treaty* in 1951 that established the European Coal and Steel Community (ECSC) with six participating countries, Belgium, Germany,

France, Italy, Luxembourg and the Netherlands, European integration has continued to expand. The initial focus of the Community was predominantly on economic cooperation and integration. By 1995 the European Economic Community (EEC) had 15 members with UK, Denmark and Ireland joining in 1973, Greece in 1981, Portugal and Spain in 1986, and Austria and Finland in 1995. In 2004 10 new countries joined: the Czech Republic, Estonia, Cyprus, Latvia, Lithuania, Hungary, Malta, Poland, Slovenia and Slovakia. Finally, in 2007, with the accession of Bulgaria and Romania, EU reached its current membership of 27 countries.

Similarly, the scope of the EU has expanded. Initially European integration was seen mainly in economic terms with an emphasis on the development of a single market. Increasingly, social policy has been seen as a necessary pre-requisite for successful economic integration. The Single European Act (1986) defined social policy as well as economic and social cohesion as new areas of the EU's powers. This was developed further in the *Treaty of the European Union* signed in Maastricht in 1992 which constituted European citizenship.

Following the United Nations (UN, 1993) resolution of the *UN Standards Rules for the Equalization of Opportunities for Persons with Disabilities*, the European Commission adopted in 1996 the Communication COM (96) 406 which promotes equal rights and non-discrimination on the basis of disability and the mainstreaming of disability issues in EU policies (for example, social policy, education and training, research, transport, telecommunications and public health). Mainstreaming refers to how social programmes should be organized; that is in education providing a system that allows disabled students to be educated in regular schools rather than in a separate provision.

Article 13 of the *Amsterdam Treaty* in 1997 is of a particular interest since it gave to the Community the power to act in order to combat discrimination based on sex, race, ethnic origin, religion or belief, disability, age or sexual orientation. Two directives were adopted in 2000. These directives were influenced by the EU gender equality legislation that has a long history. The Council Directive 2000/43/EC or 'racial equality directive' prohibits direct and indirect discrimination and harassment on grounds of racial or ethic origin and it covers the areas of employment, training and education, social security, health care, housing and access to goods and services. The Council Directive 2000/78/EC, named the 'employment equality directive', which covers *employment, occupation* and *vocational training*, prohibits direct and indirect discrimination on the grounds of religion or belief, disability, age and sexual orientation, also refers to reasonable accommodation for promoting the access of persons of disabilities to employment and training. As part of the *Renewed Social Agenda: Opportunities, Access and Solidarity in 21st Century Europe*, the European Commission adopted a proposal for a Council Directive to combat discrimination and to implement the principle of equal treatment based on religion or belief, disability, age or sexual orientation *outside the field of employment.*

The attempt to introduce an EU Constitution (Treaty Establishing a Constitution for Europe, 2004) was unsuccessful at the ratification process. The *Lisbon Treaty* (2007), which is planned to be ratified by the member states and to come into force in 2009, revisits the issue of the future of the EU, including a Charter of Fundamental rights. Article 21 (Non-discrimination) prohibiting any discrimination based on any ground such as sex, race, colour, ethnic or social origin, genetic features, language, religion or belief, political or any other opinion, membership of a national minority, property, birth, disability, age or sexual orientation.

Priestley (2007) argues that the pre-Maastricht period was characterized mainly by a 'soft' approach to social policy on disability with 'fair opportunities' as the driver and indirect intervention in the national policies related to disability focusing predominantly on employment participation. The *Maastricht Treaty* which introduced the concept of social inclusion – and social exclusion – was also the point of a 'shift in European disability policy marked by recognition of citizenship, the adoption of a more legalistic rights-based approach and the acquisition of new supranational powers of governance' (Priestley, 2007: 67).

Thus at the moment the principles of mainstreaming and anti-discrimination/ equal treatment rights inform European policy, by coexisting in some areas (employment, occupation and vocational training), while in others, for instance compulsory education, only the former applies. Mabbett (2005: 108) argues that 'mainstreaming develops non-discrimination as a programmatic rather than a justifiable right, aiming for engagement in the sphere of policy-making rather than seeking remedies for individuals'. According to her, disability organizations advocating at the European-level have reasons for endorsing mainstreaming since it introduces a 'disability perspective' across different programmes. However, the acceptance of mainstreaming would seem to have been mostly rhetorical.

 Point for reflection

> The EU social policy in general and in respect of disability in particular has evolved and expanded since the foundation of the European Community. This policy was driven by the economic development of the EU and the notion of European 'values' and 'identity'. Both mainstreaming and antidiscrimination policies are utilized in promoting equality for different groups, including disabled people. There are tensions between these two approaches to equality. Their implementation is frequently contested by each member state's approach to these issues at the level of national policy and practice.

Our discussion does suggest that there is increased interest in disability issues in the European Union's social policy, but among the questions to consider are:

1. What are the implications of linking equality to economic development?
2. Does such a link limit possibilities for inclusion to take place when equality is seen as incompatible with economic development?
3. Would politicians be justified in arguing that economic development should take precedence over social equality?

European Union social policy: special education and inclusion

The European Union has had a supportive and supplementary role in respect of national education policy of member states. The principle of subsidiarity governs education and each member state is responsible for the organization and the content of national education. However, education is seen as central in promoting economic development and social inclusion. Currently, three goals adopted by the European Council in 2001 constitute objectives for educational systems to be met by 2010:

- improving the quality and effectiveness of education and training systems;

- ensuring that they are accessible to all;

- opening up education and training to the wider world.

Cooperation and exchange between member states in promoting and implementing these policies and goals are strongly encouraged by the European Union.

European Union documents and publications in the sphere of education are characterized by an approach that is encompassing (that is, understands social inclusion as a process for achieving equality of opportunity) and group-specific (that is, focused on disability and/or special education needs). The importance of the relation between education and economic advancement is targeted and specifically linked to the promotion of social inclusion and the overcoming of exclusion. The dual role of education for economic advancement and social inclusion is presented as self-evident. This is, of course, a 'circular' argument that can be read in two ways: 'better' education will create more opportunities for employment and therefore less (social) exclusion; and 'better' education will decrease (social) exclusion and therefore more people will be able to find employment. However, the emphasis may be different in different reforms and in consequence contradictory reforms may be promoted based on the same argument.

Social inclusion/exclusion as it developed in the 1990s as a 'political-moral' ideology is justified and legitimated by a 'crisis discourse' (see, for example, Berliner and Biddle, 1995; Carr and Hartnett, 1996). This 'crisis discourse' is a twofold one: on the one hand, the educational system or components of that system (that is, teachers, schools) are seen to be 'failing' to meet national needs or priorities; on the other hand, education is represented as failing to meet the needs of a new globalized economy, which demands a 'flexible' workforce. Flexibility in this context means that individuals (or citizens) need to be educated 'for life' in order to follow the technological changes of production and, at the same time, be able to adapt to 'flexible' forms of employment.

Thus, the 'crisis discourse' questions the educational system as a whole and at the same time specific parts of it. It can be argued that this dual character of the crisis discourse gives it some credibility since education is seen both in its relation to the wider context, and at the same time the failure or success of schools is generally represented as occurring independently without reference to the wider context and the purposes of education. That is the marketization of education has taken place in a globalized economy in response to changing modes of production, employment insecurity and new forms of inclusion/exclusion. However, national policy cannot be disentangled from the localized reforms which are perceived as a response to issues and problems within that localized setting.

The statistics of special education

Statistical data are collected by the European Union under the heading of 'Special Education'. In the publication *Key Data on Education in Europe 1999–2000* (European Commission [EC], 2000) a chapter was dedicated to special education. The premise of the data analysis is that educational systems are moving from segregation (the historical beginning of special education provision) to integration. The chapter starts with the sentence that 'special education was developed in the course of the nineteenth century in order to guarantee the right of all children to education' (ibid.: 139). As we have discussed in other chapters, this is one, but not the sole, interpretation of the origins of special education.

The EC utilizes a categorization system based on three major organizational models of education for children with special educational needs (SEN). Thus the 2000 statistical report identifies the three categories as follows (ibid.: 141):

1. The first category is referred to as the 'one-track' category and includes countries that develop a policy and practice geared towards the integration of almost all pupils within mainstream education. 'Generally speaking, this type of integration is supported by a wide range of services focusing on the mainstream school. The percentage of pupils attending special (that is, separate) classes or schools is less than 1 per cent, and the children considered as having special needs do not generally constitute a large percentage of the population (less than 2 per cent)'.

2. The second category occurs in countries belonging to the 'two-track' category which cater for over 3 per cent of pupils in separate special education. The percentage of pupils with special educational needs in mainstream schools in these countries is very small.

3. Countries belonging to the third category (the 'multi-track') have a multiplicity of approaches to integration. 'They do not offer one single solution (integration in mainstream education with the support of many different services) or a choice between two options (mainstream or special education), but rather a variety of services between these two systems. The range from special multiple classes (full-time or part-time) to different forms of inter-school cooperation including 'exchange' categories (with teachers and pupils from mainstream and special schools arranging temporary or part-time exchanges). These countries sometimes have a considerable number of pupils with special educational needs and between 1 and 5 per cent of pupils in separate schools'. (ibid: 141)

Subsequent publications updating reports on special education modify both the categories and the forms of reporting data. The most recent publication *Key Data on Education in Europe 2005* (EC, 2005) dedicates only two pages to special education as part of the 'Participation' chapter.

The description of categories changes from 'track/s' of available provision in 2001 to percentage in separate setting in 2005, without explanation. Furthermore, there is a change in the tone of the publication. The previous two publications (EC, 2000; 2002) were based on the premise that there is a trend from segregated education to integration and this is a positive and desirable outcome. In fact the 2000 publication claimed that 'the situation is currently in the throes of change' with 'two-track' countries with distinct general and special education systems moving towards a 'multi-track' approach. However, by 2005 it is reported that within the special needs education field, the *desired* situation is generally agreed to be inclusion of pupils with SEN within compulsory mainstream education, although this is not universally agreed to be *appropriate* for all SEN pupils.

> It is therefore important to bear in mind that the issue of quality of education is not addressed by only considering developments in the proportion of SEN pupils who

are educated separately. *Placement in an inclusive setting does not necessarily guarantee quality provision*; conversely, *placement in a separate setting does not result in inappropriate educational provision for some pupils*. (EC, 2005: 129, emphasis added)

The above statement raises two issues. Although, arguably, there is not a straightforward relation between the setting of educational provision and the quality of education provided, this assertion applies both to regular and separate/specialized settings as inclusion is not simply a matter of setting placement. However, in arguing that in some circumstances a placement in a regular school may be 'inappropriate' we see a new assertion of an individualized approach to special education needs, according to which the 'needs' of some students cannot be met within the regular school no matter the extent of additional support.

Table 6.1 Comparison of the classification of countries based on EC (2000, 2002, 2005) categories

EC (2000)		EC (2002)		EC (2005)	
One-track (>1%)	Greece Spain Italy Portugal Sweden Norway** Cyprus*	One-track (>1%)	Greece Spain Italy Portugal Sweden Norway** Iceland**3 Cyprus*	>1%	Greece Spain Italy Portugal Iceland** Norway** Cyprus
	N=7		N=8		N=7
Two-track (<3%)	Belgium Netherlands Bulgaria* Latvia* Romania*	Two-track (N/A%)	Belgium Netherlands Romania* Malta*1	1–3%	Belgium (de)4b Netherlands Romania* Malta Denmark France Ireland Luxembourg Austria United Kingdom Liechtenstein** Lithuania Poland Slovenia Bulgaria* Sweden
	N=5		N=4		15 + Be (de)
Multi-track (1–5%)	Denmark Germany France Ireland	Multi-track (1–5%)	Denmark Germany France Ireland	<3%	Belgium (fr, nl)4a Czech Republic Germany Estonia

Table 6.1   (Continued)

EC (2000)		EC (2002)	EC (2005)
	Luxembourg	Luxembourg	Latvia
	Austria	Austria	Hungary
	Finland	Finland	Slovakia
	United Kingdom	United	Finland
	Iceland[**]	Kingdom	
	Liechtenstein[**]	Liechtenstein[**]	
	Czech Republic[*]	Czech Republic[*]	
	Estonia[*]	Estonia[*]	
	Lithuania[*]	Lithuania[*]	
	Hungary[*]	Hungary[*]	
	Poland[*]	Poland[*]	
	Slovenia[*]	Slovenia[*]	
	Slovakia[*]	Slovakia[*]	
		Bulgaria[2*]	
		Latvia[2*]	
	N=17	N=18	7 + Be (fr, nl)
Total	N=29	Total N=30	N=30

Notes:
[*]Classified as pre-accession countries at the point of publication.
[**]Countries of the European Free Trade Association which are members of the European Economic Area.
1 No data for EU (2000).
2 Change from 'two-track' to 'multi-track' between 2000 and 2002.
3 Change from 'multi-track' to 'one-track' between 2000 and 2002.
4a Belgian-French and Flemish communities.
4b Belgian-German-speaking community.
Sources:
EC (2000) *Key Data on Education in Europe 1999–2000*. Luxembourg: European Commission.
EC (2002) *Key Data on Education in Europe 2002*. Luxembourg: European Commission.
EC (2005) *Key Data on Education in Europe 2005*. Luxembourg: European Commission.

Due to the differences in the categorization between the three publications, it is difficult to draw comparisons in terms of the 'usefulness' of the different categories used. Table 6.1 gives an indication of the relation between the two different categorizations. Although the indicator of the percentage of students educated separately provides some insight into the size of special education provision, its overall use is limited. The main difference between the two categorizations is in relation to the two-track model describing two distinct systems of general and special education. It may be argued that European policy has an effect on member state policy in that respect, facilitating through the principle of mainstreaming the introduction of pathways between the two systems through the adoption of relevant legislation. It might be the case that in terms of policy, two-track systems are approaching their extinction.

〜〜 **Point for reflection**

There is limited movement between categories from the 2000 to the 2002 publication. However, the restructuring of categories in the 2005 publication results in significant change to how countries are categorized. While the number of countries with less than 1 per cent of their population in separate provision stayed relatively stable across the three publications, there is a re-shuffling between the second and third category. In the 2005 report, half the countries are represented as having between 1 and 3 per cent separate provision. Furthermore, from the eight countries with more than 3 per cent separate provision, only Germany and the two Belgian communities are from the 'old' European countries, with the remainder being countries that joined the EU in 2004.

The change in categorization between these data sets raises a number of questions:

1. Does the percentage approach to separate educational provision/inclusion reinforce the assumption that there is a group of students that cannot or should not be educated in the regular classroom?
2. What are the implications of there being approximately 2 per cent of students in separate provision for those countries that deviate from the average?
3. What implications might there be for inclusive educational policies and initiatives?

An indicator that is perhaps more useful for our analysis is the overall percentage of students recognized as having special educational needs and the percentage of those educated separately in special classes and schools. The first two of the publications referred to above provide data on this indicator, covering the data collection periods 1997–98 (EC, 2000) and 2000–01 (EC, 2002). This indicator gives an indication of the variation of assessment and categorization as well as setting of provision.

For example, Finland in 2000–01 identified 17.8 per cent of the student population as having special educational needs and 3.7 per cent of those students are educated in separate provision (EC, 2002: ch. B, p. 13). Itkonen and Jahnukainen (2007: 14) report that approximately 28 per cent of school-aged children in Finland receive special education and intensive interventions. The authors in that study argue that intensive part-time intervention at the early stages of education 'allow students with academic difficulties to master skills, to "exit" special education, or to not become identified as having disabilities' (ibid: 15). They add, however, that the prevalence of students with emotional and behaviour disabilities as well as 'other' disabilities do not exhibit a similar decrease and they remain stable across age groups. The number of students identified with special education needs and receiving additional support in Finland has followed an increased trend throughout the 1990s (Vislie, 2003). The process of providing individ-ualized additional support for students experiencing learning difficulties under the 'label' of special education in Finland may require a more sensi-tive indicator to be unpacked in terms of its outcomes for all students receiving special provision.

To give another example of the complexity of provision, 15 per cent of the school population in Iceland is identified as having special educational needs and 0.9 per cent is educated in separated provision, while in Wales 3.3 per cent is identified with SEN and 0.8 per cent is educated in separated provision. Thus, while the two systems have similar percentages of students in separate provision, the overall size of the special education sector is substantially different.

Finally, there are a number of countries such as Belgium, France, the Netherlands, Liechtenstein, Latvia, Hungary and Romania where the majority of students identified as having special educational needs are educated in separate provi-sion. On the other hand, Italy, Greece and Cyprus have substantially lower numbers of students identified with SEN and the majority is educated in sep-arate provision. It is more than simplistic to claim that one-track countries are by definition more 'inclusive' than multi-track countries, especially if using a broad understanding of inclusion. The statistics presented here refer to stu-dents identified as having special educational needs. In addition to the varia-tion of the categories of students put into this category across countries, educational systems may utilize a number of other ways for stratifying stu-dents while other students are excluded or their disrupted participation and dropping out is tolerated.

However, the existing data in special education provides no evidence of a sig-nificant turn towards inclusive practices (EC, 2005; European Agency for Development in Special Needs Education [EADSNE] 2003; Vislie, 2003). As EADSNE (2003: 16) reports, on average 2 per cent of all pupils are educated in separate settings and in the recent years 'countries with a relatively large special needs education system in segregated settings showed an ongoing increase in the percentages of pupils educated in special schools'. Despite the rhetoric of social and educational inclusion, levels of segregation stay either unchangeable or even increase.

The European Union social policy: fragmentation of educational and social inclusion

In this section we discuss three recent EU publications that refer to education and aspects of social inclusion. The first document is the Eurydice (2006) working document entitled *Specific Educational Measures to Promote all Forms of Giftedness at School in Europe*. It is a study that overviews existing definitions and provisions in 30 countries. In the introduction of the document the Council of Europe (1994) recommendation on the special educational needs of young people with exceptional potential is presented. Reference also is made to the 'risk factors' of school failure and drop out potentially experienced by gifted and talented students if their needs are not met. In our discussion we use the term 'gifted and talented', but a number of different terms are used in the countries participating in the study. According to the report, in Finland, Sweden and Norway there is no specific term in use for this group of students and the 'lack of such a term reflects a declared political commitment to avoiding any classification of the latter, especially in terms of ability' (Eurydice, 2006: 8).

Further, legislation referring to special educational needs in 10 countries includes the 'gifted and talented category', while one country, Liechtenstein, has dedicated legislation for gifted and talented students. In terms of special educational measures for this group of students, the report presents a continuum of provision with most of the countries positioned between the two extremes. At one end of the continuum there are countries that prefer a more 'selective' approach (but not at its extreme form) with specialist schools and/or a variety of special measures. The Czech Republic, Latvia and Poland belong in this group. At the other end, there is an integration model allowing for differentiation within the regular classroom and this is preferred by Finland, Sweden and Iceland, while Malta with Norway are even closer to that end of the spectrum.

Despite the similarities between systems located at different points of the continuum which broadly fit into social policy models, each country experiences unique situated circumstances. For example, Vislie (2006: 410) in an account of the historical development of special education through modernity, describes the reform of special education in Norway in 2004 as 'an attack both on special education, but also on inclusive education' with both of them being 'overruled by individualization'. Educational systems respond to EU directives and other external factors through their historical and contextual situations, and groupings in terms of their social policy traditions and characteristics, albeit helpful, can mask these differences.

Returning to the working document on 'giftedness', although it outlines the possibility of an integrated approach to differentiation to meet the needs of students within the wider diversity of their classroom, this discussion is not linked to a broader understanding of inclusion in terms of school organization and practice. This does not allow for an exploration of 'special educational needs'. Rather it is simply assumed as a given characteristic of the individual student, and not as arising from the interaction between the student and the educational system.

The second document under discussion is called *Integrating Immigrant Children into Schools in Europe* (Eurydice, 2004). The education of immigrant children has a long tradition in a number of European countries and a very brief tradition in others. This is another area where access to participation is restricted and linked to social exclusion. Immigrant children have specific linguistic, educational and cultural needs, and their status may put them and their families in vulnerable positions in their host societies. We focus our discussion on two aspects of this report: the different models of integration of immigrant students in education and inter-cultural education.

The first aspect, that of pattern of integration is discussed again in terms of two different approaches, an *integrated model* distinguished by direct integration with support provided (a) within the mainstream classroom and (b) in withdrawal from the mainstream classroom; and a *separate model* distinguished by (a) transitional support and (b) long-term support (a year or more). Further, the integrated model can be assisted by extra-curricular tuition that takes place on the school premises but outside school practices. These different approaches to the immigrant students' integration resonate with the discussion above on special educational needs and giftedness and the choice between integrated or separated arrangements.

Most educational systems provide a combination of the two approaches. Exclusively direct integration is used in Ireland, Italy and the UK (Scotland) (Eurydice, 2004), while exclusively separate provision is used in Germany and Romania (moreover a number of countries have no support measures, Latvia, Hungary, Malta and Bulgaria).

Inter-cultural education refers to the curricula opportunities provided to all students, regardless of whether they are immigrants or not, in order to engage with cultural diversity and cultural exchange and interactions. Three levels are identified: learning about cultural diversity, international dimensions and the European dimension. Only Iceland and Bulgaria do not explicitly address an inter-cultural approach in their curricula, while the other countries address one or more of the three levels. The report mentions that among the subjects that can be linked into cross-curricular areas to address inter-cultural issues are history, geography, civics, ethics and citizenship education. As Lister (1997: 43) states 'critical citizenship theory has put the spotlight on the symbiotic processes of inclusion and exclusion which form the kernel of citizenship as a concept and a practice'. It is through a broad definition of inclusion, that the fragmentation of 'groups in need of inclusion' can be transcended and that issues of inclusion/ exclusion can be seen as relevant to all participants and not simply what schools 'do' to individual or groups of students. Furthermore, it is through inclusive curricula that issues of social inclusion and exclusion, discrimination, individual differences and diversity can be debated and negotiated in schools.

The final document to be considered in this chapter is the *Early Childhood Education and Care in Europe: Tackling Social and Cultural Inequalities* (Education, Audiovisual and Culture Executive Agency, 2009). Our discussion is confined to the question of how the focus population is defined and constructed in this report. The focus is upon issues of Early Childhood Education and Care (ECEC) with an emphasis on policies geared to 'at risk children'. It adopts one of the three categories of the OECD framework, that of the disadvantages, which defines special educational needs in terms of socio-economic, cultural and/or language factors (the three categories of the OECD indicator are discussed in Chapter 8). Children experiencing special educational needs due to disability are specifically excluded from consideration here.

As with the previous documents that we have discussed, the report brings together issues of 'rights' and social exclusion, equity and efficiency, but predominantly it engages in a discussion of 'risk'. In introducing the literature review on risk factors, it argues that there are four complementary explanations for early education disadvantages among low income, ethnic minority and immigrant children:

1. An accumulation of socio-economic and psychological 'risks'.

2. A lack of stimulation of cognitive and language development in family interactions.

3. Different cultural beliefs determining parenting styles and socialization practices.

4. Linguistic and educational consequences of bilingualism.

The construction of disadvantage and inequality presented above adopts a 'deficit' model that implies that it is the individual child and his/her family environment that are deficient in managing their social and cultural characteristics (which are also perceived as deviant) to minimize or avoid 'risk'. The school then compensates for this deficit. In a Europe with increased diversity and precarious economic circumstances for an increased part of the population, pathologizing the circumstances that create social exclusion at the individual, family and community level reinforces social exclusion as a 'personal problem'.

 Point for reflection

Earlier in this chapter we described social inclusion as a 'crisis discourse'. Linked to this discourse and how it is expressed in education is the notion of 'risk'; the risk of individuals, schools and systems failing to achieve their potential. Each of the three reports discussed in this chapter refer to risk factors to which students with particular experiences or characteristics are exposed. The role of education is represented as being to intervene in students' lives to minimize risk. This leads to a fragmented and individualized approach to education. Yet, it also begs the question of whether the tension between integrated and separate provision is an inescapable one, or is it itself the consequence of an individualized and deficit approach to difference? *What kinds of inclusive programmes and curricula might move us away from such an approach?*

In this chapter we engaged with EU social policy in the area of disability, social inclusion and educational inclusion. The chapter introduced the complexities of the European Union and the European social model at the EU policy level and the implementation of social and educational policies in schools. While an increasing number of national systems endorse an 'inclusive orientation', there is little evidence that they have become less segregated or more inclusive. In fact, available statistics show that the basic categorization of separated special education (that is, systems with large special education sector), mainstreamed systems (that is, where special education services are provided mainly within the regular school) and mixed systems have not been changed or affected in any way.

In our discussion we used a broad definition of inclusion, compatible to some extent with social inclusion. On the other hand, we have challenged the fragmentation of the school population into distinct groups that some of them are deemed as needing individual interventions to be included. We offered a number of examples of how these interventions as add-ons to

existing practices are presented in a continuum of integrated–separated provision, but not very often as 'mainstreamed' processes.

 Summary

The EU is a supranational organization that influences the development of policies in member states. In the past 10 years the EU has become more concerned with social policy. This chapter looked at three different examples of social policy. The development of EU social policy in the area of disability, the existing special education arrangements and statistics, and policy documents related to diverse issues of social and educational inclusion were presented. In doing so we have sought to highlight how social and educational inclusion define and respond to issues of diversity, individual difference, equality and efficiency. We have argued that there are tensions in EU social policy and that these should not be seen independently from the wider context of social and educational inclusion within the EU, the proposed range of 'solutions' to the problem of social exclusion and the local historical and political contexts within which policy and practice are developed within individual member states.

 Discussion questions

- Is there any relation between European Union policies of social inclusion and inclusive education?
- What are the implications of the European Union policies that relate to disability for schools and disabled students?
- Have European Union inclusive polices an effect on different national educational systems?
- Are these policies effective in promoting a 'common definition' of inclusion?

Further reading

The European Agency for Development in Special Needs Education (2003) *Special Needs Education in Europe: Thematic Publication*. Brussels: EADSNE.

Mabbett, D. (2005) 'The development of rights-based social policy in the European Union: the example of disability rights', *Journal of Common Market Studies*, 43(1): 97–120.

Priestly, M. (2007) 'In search of European disability policy: between national and global', *European Journal of Disability Research*, 1(1): 61–74.

Vislie, L. (2003) 'From integration to inclusion; focusing global trends and changes in the western European societies', *European Journal of Special Needs Education*, 18(1): 17–35.

Notes

1. The European Union is a complex organization including numerous institutions and bodies. In a simplistic presentation the EU has two main legislative bodies, the European Parliament and the European Council, one executive body, the European Commission, and one judiciary, the Court of Justices.

2. Further information about the Treaties discussed in this section, as well as those omitted, can be found in the European Parliament's (2009) *Fact Sheets on the European Union*.

Section 3

From Policy to Practice

In the third section of our book we consider the nature of inclusive practices and look at the translation of policy into practice at the school level. We review many of the positive changes in school practices that have drawn on the ideas and policies of inclusive education but also consider the impact of a range of competing educational drivers on the possibilities for realizing inclusive educational goals in school practice. In the developing world there has been an upsurge of interventions at the school and classroom level designed to create more inclusive environments. As discussed in previous chapters, the meaning of 'inclusion' in the developing world is highly contested and often critically influenced by perspectives from the developed world. These are easily translated into proselytizing interventions that are insensitive to local cultural, social and economic contexts, and which can lead to inclusive education as a technical 'fix' for wider inequalities arising within a post-colonial environment.

Making Inclusion Special: A Case Study of English Policy Contradictions

Chapter overview

In England, until recently, the focus of special educational policy was restricted either to developing special systems and procedures of education for children with disabilities and/or learning difficulties, or to the promotion of policies whereby these children would be 'integrated' into the ordinary school. Now, the dominant discourse in special education is one characterized by 'inclusion'. The idea of 'inclusion', however, suggests something that goes beyond simply accessing mainstream education, yet its precise meaning is by no means clear. Perhaps conveniently, it is a concept that blurs the edges of social policy with a feel-good rhetoric that no one could be opposed to. But what does it really mean to have an education system that is 'inclusive'? Who is thought to be excluded and in what sense? If education should be inclusive, then what practices is it contesting, what common values is it advocating, and by what criteria should its successes be judged? This chapter considers the development of policies of 'inclusion' in the English education system, particularly since the major post-Second World War welfare reforms. It argues that these reforms were characterized by contradictions that have continued to influence the more recent policy initiatives around inclusive education. These contradictions are evidenced by the very limited progress that has been made in moving away from conceptualizations of educational disadvantage in terms of individual deficits. At a deeper level, the policy of inclusion reflects trends in our global society towards the normalization and homogenization of the anti-democratic values that marginalize those outside the mainstream or who stand 'against the stream'.

Special education is generally seen as a charitable, humanitarian concern rather than as a political issue. Throughout its history, this humanitarian language, or discourse as it is sometimes referred to, has been significant for securing additional resources for children experiencing difficulties within the mainstream education system, or who have been excluded altogether from that system. Yet, beneath the surface of this humanitarianism there have always been rumblings of a 'dark side' to special education – a view that the system is used to manage children who are troublesome to their schools and teachers.

The idea of inclusive education in England over the past decade has replaced the old language of special education, yet this change of language has masked a much more complicated and ambiguous policy framework. The importance of mainstream schooling has been at the centre of inclusive education policy with an emphasis upon the provision of high-quality education for all and on the responsibility shared by all teachers for children with special needs. Yet, in other respects the vision of inclusion has retained some very traditional approaches towards special education and for this reason reinforced some of the less enlightened views of children who experience difficulties with learning.

In this chapter we look at the Labour government's early Green Paper on special and inclusive schooling, *Excellence for All Children* (DfES, 1997b) which provided the framework for reforms to the system together with three key initiatives on inclusive education:

- the 2001 *Revised Code of Practice* (DfES, 2001);

- the *Special Educational Needs and Disability Act* (HMSO, 2001);

- the SEN Strategy, *Removing Barriers to Achievement* (DfES, 2004), which aims to bring special educational services under the broader strategy of child protection.

Despite the rhetoric of 'inclusion' it would be misleading to represent 1997 as a turning point for 'inclusive education'. The statistics on the identification, statementing and placement of children with special educational needs during the period of New Labour's term of office do not suggest any radical transformation of practice. Indeed, policy on inclusive education has led to the creation of a new special educational 'industry' under the banner of 'inclusion'.

Year zero: the end of ideology and beginning of an inclusive society?

Robin Alexander (2003), writing in the *Times Educational Supplement*, argued that for the new Labour government 1997 represented 'year zero' in education 'in which history and enlightenment began'. The 'enlightenment' of educational policy was founded upon the view that school-effectiveness research had shown how school improvement was possible. The language of individual pupil needs was replaced by a policy focused upon failing schools and the actions required to transform institutional failure into success and by this means into individual pupil achievement. The White Paper *Excellence in Education* (DfEE, 1997a) set out the broad agenda of the government as it started upon an educational 'crusade'. Emphasis was placed upon the improvement of 'standards' and the accountability of schools, setting out six policy principles:

- Education will be at the heart of the government.

- Policies will benefit the many, not just the few.

- The focus will be on standards in schools, not the structure of the school system.

- We will intervene in underperforming schools and celebrate the successful.

- There will be zero tolerance of underperformance.

- Government will work in partnership with all those committed to raising standards.

Shortly after publication of this document the government brought out its consultation paper *Excellence for All Children: Meeting Special Educational Needs* (DfEE, 1997b), which signalled its commitment to improving the quality of education for children with special educational needs.

The then Secretary of State for Education David Blunkett, made clear in his Foreword to this special education policy paper that, 'There is nothing more important to the Government than raising the standards children achieve in our schools' and this vision of school improvement and rising standards was for children with special educational needs 'an inclusive vision' (DfEE, 1997b: 4). He expressed concern that mainstream schools were identifying 18 per cent of their children as having special educational needs and almost 3 per cent of children had statutory statements of special educational needs which set out additional special educational provision that they required. For Blunkett, this said something very telling about the quality of education being provided within the mainstream school sector.

Six principles guiding the new thinking on inclusive education

- High expectations for all children, including those with special educational needs.

- Promotion of the inclusion of children with special educational needs within mainstream schooling wherever possible.

(Continued)

(Continued)

- Commitment to providing parents of children with special educational needs with effective services from the full range of local services and voluntary agencies.

- Value for money with a shift of resources from expensive remediation to cost-effective prevention and early intervention.

- Boosting opportunities for staff development in special education.

- Local provision for special education based upon a partnership of all those with a contribution to make.

The target-setting agenda of the first term of the New Labour government has been well documented, as have some of the spectacular failures to meet the targets set. This document was no exception. A total of 31 policy targets were set for inclusive education with an implementation date of no later than 2002. As the government came to recognize, targets are a hostage to fortune and few of these targets were met. A dynamic programme of transformation appeared to have been put in place but in practice very little changed.

The targets set out in *Excellence for All Children* are grouped into eight sections which can be summarized as follows: improving efficiency to reduce expenditure; maximizing parental involvement and therefore responsibility; refining early assessment procedures to reduce statementing; encouraging integration of children with special educational needs in mainstream schools; improving national and regional planning and support for children with special educational needs; training teachers and support staff; maximizing interagency collaboration; and building teacher skills and support systems for managing pupils with emotional and behavioural difficulties. Nowhere did the strategy talk about the barriers that create educational disadvantage; nowhere does it talk about the institutional and social discrimination experienced by pupils from certain minority groups (for example, children of Caribbean heritage and children of Irish heritage, to name but two); nowhere does it talk about the principles of an inclusive society and the role of education as a tool of social policy for supporting social cohesion and inclusion. The basic approach remained unchanged.

There was little recognition of the wider social barriers that inhibited inclusion within the environment of mainstream education. Barriers that were recognized were those of low expectations and standards. The wider context of discrimination, segregation and exclusion were largely ignored. At the same time, children were often cut adrift in a mainstream system that did not have the resources and skills to support them and where they were frequently unwanted. The system that resulted from the government's reform of special education was frequently a 'postcode lottery', with the availability and quality of educational support for children experiencing difficulties varying dramatically across the country.

In the next section we consider the three specific initiatives that were introduced during this period:

- the *Special Educational Needs Code of Practice* (DfES, 2001)

- the 2001 *Special Educational Needs and Disability Act* (HMSO, 2001)

- the 2004 Strategy for SEN, *Removing Barriers to Achievement* (DfES, 2004).

A new policy framework

A new code of practice

The 2001 *Code of Practice* was not in itself new. It revised the existing *Code of Practice on the Identification and Assessment of Special Educational Needs* introduced by the previous Conservative government in 1994 (DfE, 1994). However, the new Code replaced a five-stage assessment process with two pre-statutory stages: 'School Action' and 'School Action Plus'. The former was to be initiated where there is evidence of poor progress linked to emotional and behavioural difficulties, sensory or physical problems, or communication difficulties, despite the child having received normal differentiated learning opportunities in the classroom. The action to be taken was to be specified in an individual education plan. School Action Plus involves a request for help from external services and follows upon continued lack of progress on the part of the child, despite the measures taken at the School Action stage. Whereas, in the past, a referral of a child with special educational needs to outside agencies generally resulted in a statement of special educational needs and, frequently, placement in a special school, the *Code of Practice* was designed to avoid this by ensuring a clear record of assessment, intervention and review at each stage. By implementing such procedures it was intended to avoid the crisis management of children who experience difficulties with learning.

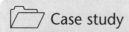 Case study

The background to reform

- 1978: *The Warnock Report* recommended the abolition of categories of special educational needs, and understanding these as being on a continuum affected by school and family circumstances as well as factors to do with the child
- 1981: *Education Act* turned many of the Warnock recommendations into legislation and introduced a new assessment (statementing) procedure for children with special educational needs
- 1993: *Education Act* established the need for a Code of Practice to guide assessment, focused in particular upon early identification and intervention where children were experiencing difficulties in school
- 1994: *Code of Practice* introduced a five-stage procedure ranging from initial classroom monitoring to statutory assessment and created the new role in each school of the Special Educational Needs Co-ordinator (SENCO) with responsibility for developing individual education plans (IEPs) which were to include information on such things as short-term targets, teaching strategies, special resources, review dates, and so on.

One of the major impacts of the *Code of Practice* has been to give greater responsibility to mainstream schools and to ordinary classroom teachers for pupils with special educational needs. Yet, teachers may be encouraged to represent different sorts of issues under the banner of special educational needs simply because the Code provides a convenient system for organizing the management of pupils who experience difficulties with learning and behaviour in their schools. Deeper-seated problems such as bullying and discrimination can easily be reconstructed under the procedures of the Code as individualized learning and behaviour deficits. In this way, the Code may perpetuate long-standing and institutionally embedded practices such as racial and gender stereotyping which lead to distortions in the gender and racial profiling of special educational needs.

Revisions to the *Code of Practice* introduced by New Labour have done nothing to address these disturbing features associated with the 'distribution' of special educational needs. Indeed, it could be argued that in some respects these features have become more damaging with the emphasis placed upon rhetoric about children's involvement in decision-making. Thus, the revised *Code of Practice* (section 3:2) states that children and young people with special educational needs 'have a unique knowledge of their own needs and circumstances and their own views about what sort of help they would like to help them make the most of their education'. Section 3:3 says that these perceptions and experiences 'can be invaluable to professionals in reaching decisions'. There is no reference to procedures for protecting children's rights against discriminatory practices that may arise from the process of assessment itself. The apparently 'inclusive' principle of children's involvement in decision-making is subordinated to the practical value of the child's involvement for those professionals who are managing the child's learning. At root, the rhetoric of inclusion is based upon the assumption that to be 'just' the education system must accommodate children whose individual disadvantages place them at risk of exclusion. It palpably fails to appreciate how the language of 'special educational needs' may be a socially constructed response by adults to troublesome behaviour that is located in wider-reaching social inequalities. In other words, ironically, it fails to appreciate how the language and policies of inclusion, as currently represented in educational policy, can be part of the problem and not part of the solution.

The 2001 Special Educational Needs and Disability Act

At first sight, a much wider reconceptualization of special educational needs is suggested by the 2001 *Special Educational Needs and Disability Act* (HMSO, 2001). This Act makes discrimination against disabled students unlawful. Thus, a duty is placed on schools not to discriminate against disabled pupils, either in the provision of education and associated services or in respect of admission to and exclusion from mainstream schooling. Section 316 of the Act states that a child who has a statement of special educational needs must be educated in the mainstream school unless this would be incompatible with (a) the wishes of the child's parents or, (b) the provision of efficient education for other children. Mainstream education cannot be refused on the grounds that the child's needs cannot be provided for within the mainstream sector. However, mainstream education can be refused on grounds that the educational interests of other children would be adversely affected by the presence of a disabled child, and this continues a qualification on inclusion that has a long legislative history.

Government policies on special education have historically shied away from linking special educational needs to the politics of disability. For this reason, the 2001 *Special Educational Needs and Disability Act* is significant. It takes forward a position long advocated by the Disabled People's Movement but it is one that in the past has been largely ignored by politicians and professional agencies working with children in educational settings.

For disability activists, there have been two broad arguments in favour of understanding inclusive policies in education in the context of society. First, disability, including learning difficulty, is a social construction; that is, it is a product of the relationship between different social groups in society and the relative power that they exercise in influencing the way the world appears to be. On this argument, impairment does not of itself give rise to disadvantage and social exclusion. Physical and mental impairments reflect the diversity of the human condition. What turns impairments into disabilities is the discrimination experienced by those with impairments. Special education, and particularly segregated special education, contributes to the oppression of disabled people in the wider society. The second argument advanced by disability activists has been that there should be a focus upon removing the barriers that prevent disabled people participating in social life. These barriers include those barring physical access to social spaces as well as the discriminatory practices of public policy and private prejudice. These two aspects are inextricably linked and this has informed the writing of a new generation of disability activists and inclusive education theorists.

The disability legislation introduced by the Labour government in the UK has hardly drawn upon this rich critical tradition. Rather it has focused on issues of physical access to public spaces. Legislation in this area is, of course, to be welcomed and removing physical barriers to access does represent an ambitious and enlightened approach. Yet, the policy implies a technical solution to the problem of how to achieve educational equity. It suggests that if only disabled people could physically access educational spaces the barriers to participation would be dissolved. At best this is idealistic. The radical thrust of the argument of disability activists, that disability is not a product of impairment but rather a social act of discrimination embedded in the power relations of society, is muted. The wider social question of why discrimination and disadvantage are so embedded in the system is lost in legislation that represents inclusion in terms of 'impairment friendly' schooling. Similarly there is no consideration of how the relations of power that support discrimination against disabled people can be transformed as a necessary basis for an inclusive society.

Historically, special education has been characterized by the pathologizing of young people who are represented as troublesome. The analysis of the processes and mechanism of exclusion by the disability movement helps to explain the 'disablement' of people in terms of the relationship between impairments, social class, gender and ethnicity. The most important contribution of the disability movement to the framing of debates about inclusive education has been to politicize disablement in terms of these broader processes of cultural representation and social exclusion. A policy promoting inclusive education that remains constrained by the goal of assimilating those with impairments into mainstream schools without addressing the exclusionary character of a disabling society is doomed to reinforce the very exclusionary process that it seeks to overcome.

'Removing barriers to achievement': the government's strategy for SEN

Another government initiative in support of inclusive schooling has been the strategy for SEN, *Removing Barriers to Achievement* (DfES, 2004). The significance of this strategy was that it placed special education within the broader policy initiative of the Green Paper *Every Child Matters* (DfES, 2003) and as such offered the most complete articulation of inclusive education policy within the Labour government's wider ideological vision of an inclusive society. *Every Child Matters* speaks to a commitment to reform children's services to prevent vulnerable children falling through the cracks between different services and the need to recognize that 'child protection cannot be separated from policies to improve children's lives as a whole' (DfES, 2003: 5). The government's strategy for SEN attempts to represent inclusive education within a similar framework of child protection by targeting attention toward four areas of activity. These are:

- Early intervention – to ensure that children who have difficulties learning receive the help they need as soon as possible and that parents of children with special educational needs and disabilities have access to suitable childcare.

- Removing barriers to learning – by embedding inclusive practice in every school and early years settings.

- Raising expectations and achievement – by developing teachers' skills and strategies for meeting the needs of children with SEN and sharpening the focus on the progress children make.

- Delivering improvements in partnership – taking a hands-on approach to improvements so that parents can be confident that their child will get the education they need.

Pursuing this child protection model of inclusion, the strategy for SEN locates special educational interventions in relation to 'risk factors' associated with educational failure, community breakdown, parenting inadequacies, school disorganization and individual and/or peer group difficulties. These risk factors have been widely proclaimed as giving rise to concerns for the welfare of young people across the domains of education, health, social welfare and youth justice, and have influenced the promotion of an interventionist strategy of risk reduction to be delivered by cross-agency childhood services. It is argued that elimination of the disadvantages of poverty can be achieved through early interventions with children because the technical skill exists to identify and target those most at risk. Therefore the reduction of poverty and disadvantage is represented as possible through technical solutions aimed at the individual child. However, what is lacking in this approach is any theorization of the ways in which risks are situated by the social structure of cultural and social relationships through which certain individual identities may be seen as 'normal' or 'abnormal'. An illusion of scientific objectivity is also created which implies that these risks and the likelihood of their effect upon future behaviour can be measured and therefore controlled by appropriate early interventions.

 Points for reflection

How important is ideology in policy about inclusive education?
What are the strengths and weakness of the following arguments?

- Poverty is the underlying cause of educational disadvantage.
- The effects of poverty can be transformed through social interventions aimed at those most at risk.
- We now have the technical skill to maximize the impact of such interventions.

Implicit in the first two of these claims seems to be a view that poverty is a consequence of the inadequacies of those individuals who are placed at risk by it. If this is not what is being claimed then what would be the purpose of intervening at the individual level rather than at the macroeconomic level to reduce poverty and its effects?

Are more children included?

The impact of these policy changes over the past 10 years or so in England are mixed. According the government's own figures (DCSF, 2008) there has been a steady and significant decline year on year since 1997 in the number of pupils in England receiving statements of special education for the first time: from 35,650 to 23,510. However, the percentage of those who were placed in the mainstream school system has declined only slightly from 71 per cent in 1997 to 69 per cent in 2007. Whereas the number of primary school children with statements has remained static at around 100,000 the number of secondary school pupils with statements has declined by about 20,000. When one allows for demographic changes, however, the percentage of pupils with statements of special education in England has remained fairly static (increasing from 2.5 per cent in 1994 to a peak of 3.1 per cent in 2001 and then declining to 2.8 per cent in 2008). Yet, these figures conceal more worrying indications of the failure of inclusive schooling to be realized. Apart from wide local variations in statementing and placement policies that have been a characteristic of the special education system throughout its history, there continue to be significant differences in statementing practice between the primary and secondary sectors. In 2008, 2 per cent of secondary school pupils had statements compared with 1.4 per cent of primary pupils. This is despite 18.1 per cent of primary pupils compared to 17.8 per cent of secondary pupils being formally identified as having special educational needs without going through the statementing process. Gender differences show the most striking disparities, with boys accounting for over 70 per cent of all statemented pupils while differences between ethnic groups continue to be pronounced despite a long history of concern about discrimination and institutional racism. For example, Travellers of Irish heritage and Roma/Gypsy children have the highest percentage of children with statements of special educational needs. School differences also suggest that little has changed since 25 years ago when attention was first drawn to this by a number of ground-breaking studies on school effectiveness (Rutter et al., 1979). Interestingly, the extensive school effectiveness literature that followed Rutter's seminal study has largely focused upon government preoccupations with academic achievement rather than upon what is perhaps more illuminative from the standpoint of inclusive schooling, namely, the social and affective dimensions of children's experiences of schooling.

The statistics suggest that very little has changed, not only over the past 10 years, but over the past 30 years since the Warnock Report first advocated the abolition of categories of special educational need and movement towards a more inclusive system based upon a continuum of needs which were themselves significantly related to the quality of education being received. More importantly, special education continues to fulfil its traditional function vis-à-vis the mainstream sector of containing troublesome individuals and depoliticizing educational failure through the technologies of measurement and exclusion.

Is the education system more inclusive?

Special educational needs continues to be a label that excuses the failure of the system to address the aspirations, dignity and human worth of so many young people. Herein lies one of the most fundamental contradictions at the heart of the Labour government's educational policy. The policy of inclusion is aimed at promoting equity but does so by establishing a narrow understanding of normality (academic achievement) which becomes the measure of successful interventions. The aim of inclusive education therefore becomes one of assimilation to that normality and in doing so implicitly operates to regulate the lives of those people who are disabled by their lack of utilitarian value within the social relations of society as currently constituted. The narrative of inclusion that features so strongly in the English social policy agenda leaves little room for alternative educational values and goals to be formulated, debated and pursued.

Government policy has been focused on increasing state intervention into the lives of individuals and families who are seen as 'failing' or 'dysfunctional' based upon beliefs about the moral importance of early intervention and prevention and the technical possibilities that science creates for the policy-maker and implementer. State intervention in the governance of children, families, schools and communities who are deemed to be potentially problematic is legitimated on the basis of moral beliefs in pathologies of risk for which technical solutions of risk management can be specified under the ideological formulation of an inclusive society. The process of educational assessment is transformed from a formative and educative process into a risk management system. On the one hand, failure is conceptualized entirely in moral terms as the consequence of individual, family, community and/or school inadequacies. On the other hand, a technical solution to these moral deficiencies is proposed, which involves early identification of at-risk populations on the basis of risk factors 'known' to correlate with the likelihood of failure or antisocial behaviour in the future. Thus, the idea of inclusive education is used to justify the growth of surveillance and management of troublesome populations based on the assumption that special educational needs are an outcome of dysfunctional individuals and communities, and that these individuals can be identified through an assessment process determined by experts. Nikolas Rose (1999: 134) has described this process as one in which 'The soul of the young person has become the object of government through expertise'. The 'science' that defines inclusion is represented as neutral in relation to the contested beliefs and values that give meaning and relevance to ideas of normality and social order. In practice, the linking of 'inclusion' to the science of 'risk assessment' supports a privatized rhetoric of individual responsibility and risk management, replacing 'need' and equity as the core principles of educational and social policy.

☐ Summary

The Labour government in the UK has pursued a vigorous agenda around the issues of social and educational inclusion. At one level it has challenged traditional views of special educational needs as individual deficits by focusing upon the role of schools in achievement of opportunities for all children. Yet, this new approach to inclusive education has been led by a discourse of children at risk which has done little to scrutinize the values of educational inclusion and how its outcomes may be re-thought. The government's inclusive educational policy has rested upon an uncritical view of 'normality' that has reinforced the traditional view of special education as being concerned with the assimilation of those experiencing difficulties into the mainstream with no attention to how the mainstream values and practices of society and its education system themselves lead to exclusion.

 Discussion questions

- Are moral questions important for the way society works with children who are different for the 'norm'? What would an ethical approach to inclusion involve?
- Should inclusive education be primarily concerned with access to equal opportunities or do we need to recognize that the different experiences and needs of different people require society itself to think differently about the meaning of inclusion?
- Does policy really make any difference or is it all talk?
- Can we apply technical solutions to social problems? What would this imply for our understanding of ethics and politics?

Further reading

Armstrong, D. (2004) 'A risky business? Research, policy, governmentality and youth offending', *Youth Justice*, 4(2): 100–16.

Department for Education and Employment (DfEE) (1997b) *Excellence for All Children: Meeting Special Educational Needs*. London: DfEE.

Dyson, A. (2001) 'Special needs education as the way to equity: an alternative approach?', *Support for Learning*, 16(3): 99–104.

Mitchell, D. (2008) *Contextualizing Inclusive Education*. London: Routledge.

Oliver, M. and Barnes, C. (1998) *Disabled People and Social Policy: From Exclusion to Inclusion*. London: Longman.

8

From Policy to Practice: Defining Inclusion in Schools

Chapter overview

In the past 20 years various policies, practices and initiatives aimed at developing inclusive schools have been developed and implemented. In addition, research has been trying to identify the characteristics of 'inclusive' schools. How can inclusion be achieved in a practical sense? Are there any schools that are inclusive? If yes, can inclusion be sustained? This chapter acknowledges the commitment of many educational authorities, schools, teachers and other personnel and parents to inclusive philosophy, principles and practices. In one sense, this chapter is a celebration of the achievements of the past 30 years in the area of inclusive education. At the same time this chapter is a cautionary tale of the limitations of inclusive policies and practices. Previous chapters have discussed how the effects of competing educational reforms, especially those geared towards schools' performance and measurable outcomes, in combination with the dominance of a deficit model approach in special education funding and organization of available services, limit *the possibility for inclusion*. In this chapter, the three-tiered model of special services provision at the school-level is examined. This model distinguishes between universal, targeted and individualized provision. It is argued that the distinction between different levels of provision in terms of focus, intensity and, in some cases, setting is neither inclusive nor exclusive; their inclusive or exclusive potential depends on whether this is part of an orchestrated attempt to make schools more inclusive or if it is a way of managing students by minimizing disruption in regular classrooms.

The inclusive potential of schools depends in large part on whether an orchestrated attempt is made at a system level to make schools more inclusive or whether they are instead structured in such a way as to manage students by minimizing disruption in regular classrooms. Moreover, both the intent of schools towards becoming more inclusive and the extent to which this is achieved cannot be seen in isolation from the question of whether the educational systems in which they are located are themselves geared to becoming more inclusive.

Decision-making in educational policy and practice can be understood as underpinned by a three-tiered model which operates at many different levels. We use the *principle of differentiation* as an analytical tool to discuss the ways that provision and support are differentiated for different purposes and different groups of students. From here we are then able to explore two continua that are commonly found within educational systems: the *continuum of achievement* and the *continuum of support*.

The principle of differentiation

The principle of differentiation is of central importance for understanding arrangements of provision in an education system. Students, schools, programmes, curriculum, learning and teaching, and so on are frequently differentiated for some groups or for individual students. In other words, differentiation is concerned with delivering education in different sorts of ways for 'different' sorts of student. Some ways of separating students in educational systems (for example, by age, in primary and secondary education) are so common that most of the time they are taken for granted in a common-sense way, as the 'natural' way of doing things. For example, all students need to be able to have access to the school physical environment and the resources that they use. In some cases specific arrangements for groups of students are made to increase accessibility. In primary schools, for instance, students attending the pre-school, nursery or kindergarten classes may have furniture and physical environment arrangements that are more accessible to them and which are different from those for older students in the school. In many educational systems this accessibility differentiation is established to the extent that is not seen as differentiation but as standard practice. While for the most part the wider physical environment is not designed and built with the purpose of being accessible to young children, schools where there are young children are generally designed and built so that they will be accessible to those children. However, this is not an accidental fact. Understanding of the significance of access for young children resulted in an awareness and acknowledgement of their needs in a number of areas (for example, education, architecture, planning regulations, furniture designing and manufacturing, and so on).

For some students, for example, physically disabled or blind students, arrangements may be required to ensure their access to the physical environment and resources. These arrangements ensure that these students have the same access to educational opportunities by the provision of specialist facilities, resources and support so that the quality of education meets what is perceived to be an acceptable standard practice. Issues of accessibility for disabled students have indeed started to inform school design in a number of countries. However, since most schools have not been designed to be accessible, the accessibility issue is raised when a student enrolled or wishing to enrol in a school faces barriers that prevent access to educational opportunities. Any changes to the actual physical environment and how it is organized will take place in order to extend standard practice to that student.

Promoting the right of accessing services on an equal basis to that experienced by people without a disability is what anti-discrimination legislation such as the *Convention on the Rights of Persons with Disabilities* (UN, 2006) and as the *Americans with Disabilities Act* (1990), the Australian *Disability Discrimination Act* (1992) and the UK *Disability Discrimination Acts* 1995 and 2005, aim to ensure. However, anti-discrimination legislation raises some issues in terms of how the principle of differentiation is understood. Although in the example above it is the standard practice that is extended to the student, albeit in a different way or through different means, it is the disabled person that becomes the centre of the process.

First, the disabled person needs to prove that they fit within the definition of disability used in a specific discrimination act. This requires the acceptance of a 'label' of disability and thus reinforces an individual and medical approach. The onus to demonstrate that appropriate adjustments are not in place is also placed on the disabled person and any process of complaining, appealing or of litigation is also initiated by the disabled person. Thus, without minimizing the importance of anti-discrimination legislation, as Barnes and Mercer (2004: 122) argue 'there is also criticism that the legal route lead to long, drawn-out, costly court actions that downgrade collective political struggles, and ignore the social and political location of the legal system'. On the other hand, as Clements and Read (2008: 13) comment the articulation of the disability experience in the language of human rights law creates a different 'value system' which the additional benefits 'of the advantage of a distinct power base – separate from that of the medical profession, the Treasury, the family and the church – and the expectation of enforceable remedies'.

Despite the limitations of anti-discrimination legislation, in those contexts where it has been adopted it has become an integral part of the ways that the differentiation principle is perceived and acted upon. Anti-discrimination disability legislation becomes central in discussions of equality and equity about how resources are differentiated for all or some individuals and regarding what constitutes standard, appropriate and reasonable provision. This discussion is informed by what the expected and desired outcomes of education are and how these outcomes can be facilitated; these refer to the continua of achievement and support and how they relate to each other. Thus different understandings of the role of the school and of education and the ways that schools are organized which permit or inhibit the ways in which differentiation may take place in the regular classroom and the regular school have an effect on the ways that the differentiation principle can be implemented in different educational systems.

The call for inclusive education systems and programmes as expressed in *The Salamanca Statement* (UNESCO, 1994) and the *Convention on the Rights of Persons with Disabilities* (UN, 2006), is based upon a human rights agenda that informs educational policy. Although the articulation of specific human rights is envisaged as uniform across different educational systems (that is, countries and systems cannot pick the rights that they want to implement), the implementation of these rights takes place within the traditions, realities and aspirations of each educational system. It is within the parameters of a specific education context that a 'right' is realized and at the same time the realization of this right affects or alters the relationships between these parameters. Again this is an example of differentiation.

The continua of achievement and support

Educational systems set specific expectations and goals for students in terms of their academic, physical, social and emotional development. For example, in terms of academic outcomes, many educational systems operate under the presumption that all (or almost all) students can reach certain educational outcomes at specific points during their educational career and that a part of the student body can reach a high-level or high-order achievement in these educational outcomes, with some students even pushing the boundaries of what would be expected for most students. This can be called the *continuum of achievement*. Common understandings about students' abilities, students' characteristics and background (for example, gender, race, socio-economic and cultural background), and of the role and scope of schooling and its influence upon different educational systems at different historical points, explain, justify and construct this continuum. The analysis in Chapter 2 of the English tripartite system is an example of this continuum of achievement and how it leads to differentiated educational provision resulting in different educational and life outcomes for different groups of students based on their performance on an academic examination at a specific point of their educational career.

At the same time, groups or individual students may be identified as having needs that are not met by the provision available to all students. These needs require additional support for them to participate in the educational system. This support is organized in terms of special services provision and in many systems is organized across levels of needs. There are different ways to categorize support and its allocation. One issue identified in the literature is that of 'equivalence' of different types of support used in different educational systems. The OECD (2003) developed an indicator that aims to overcome some of the conceptual problems of equivalence and to extend the concept of 'inclusion'. The basis of the indicator is any additional provision received by students over and above the general 'standard' provision, in order for them to access the curriculum. Three cross-national categories of students receiving such provision are distinguished.

1. Students whose needs are related to a 'substantial normative argument' (for example, sensory disabilities, severe learning disabilities and multiple disabilities).

2. Students whose needs cannot be attributed to specific factors.

3. Students whose needs are related to socio-economic, cultural and/or linguistic factors.

This approach of constructing 'special/additional' provision uses a broad understanding of inclusion. However, it is problematic for a number of reasons. The relation between 'needs' and additional provision is not a simple one. As Armstrong (1995: 132) argues: 'By defining children's needs in terms of resources those needs are individualized, inhibiting consideration of the context in which they occur, a context which includes the expectations and needs of those who request and carry out the assessment.'

Thomas and Loxley (2001) discuss how the concept of 'need' is constructed in relation to 'difficult behaviour in school'. Specific behaviours are translated into a student's need to be met, while it is the need of the school for 'order' that is actually met in this process. In this way 'an institutional need for order is transformed to a child's emotional need' (ibid.: 52). In meeting the student's needs, a variety of interventions (educational, psychological, social and medical) may be utilized. These interventions constitute part of the additional support provided to the student. The additional support provided may diversify in alternative paths of provision that take the student outside the mainstream classroom and school, removing in the process the need or 'problem' of the student.

Although the three OECD categories of students for which additional provision is required when seen together may be perceived as articulating a broad understanding of 'inclusion', the fragmentation of the three categories based on the 'cause' of need reinforces an individual approach which as Florian et al. (2006: 40) argue is 'one-dimensional and refer to categorically distinct groups'.

The OECD categorization of additional education support has two parts: in terms of the group of students receiving this support, and the setting where this support is provided. In relation to the latter, *a continuum of setting provision* is used. This is an example of a three-tiered model of location and it includes special schools, special classes in regular schools and regular classes. In addition to the continuum of setting provision, a commonly used categorization of support is that in which provision is seen as part of a *continuum of support* which include universal, targeted or directed, and individualized provision. A continuum of support may refer to all students, groups of students or individual students.

Two examples of the continuum of support

Literacy support

- All students have access to literacy instruction.

- Some students have access to additional literacy support for a short period of time (for example, remedial literacy programmes) targeting individuals (or groups with similar characteristics) performing below the expected level. This support is integral and continuing provision in the school.

- Individual students require access to intensive literacy support and in certain cases to alternative arrangements (for example, curriculum accommodations). These are tailored and organized according to the individual's needs. In some cases the school does not have provisions in place prior to the enrolment of student that the provisions are required.

Students with a home language different to the language of instruction in schools

- All students with a home language different to the one used for instruction in school *are entitled* to support provision. This provision is not available to students with the same home language as the one spoken at school. Entitlement means that students should have access to support structures if they need them.

- Some students will have access to support services available in schools for a period of time if their performance in the language of instruction is below that that is considered necessary for participating in learning.

- Individual students, due to their specific needs (which may also be presented in combination with other needs that are not due to them coming from a home language different to the language of instruction), may require support services that extend for longer or which are more intense.

The continuum of support is context specific. In the first example, for instance, what is understood by literacy support is differentiated in primary and secondary education or in relation to the dominant approach to literacy

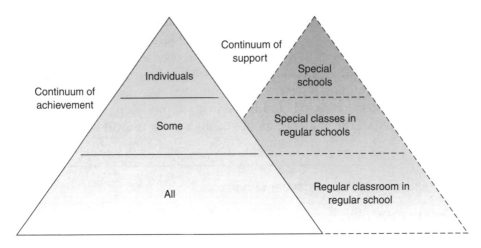

Figure 8.1 Continua of achievement and support

instruction, and so on. In the second example the understanding of what it means to be a student with a home language different to the language of instruction is not independent of the proportion of the population that belongs in this category, the number of languages that are widely used other than that of school instruction or whether the school system is bilingual.

Very often the continuum of support is represented as a triangle. At the base of the triangle there is universal support for all students, a level up there is targeted/directed support for a proportion of the students and, finally, at the top of the triangle there is individualized support as per individual needs. A similar triangle can be constructed for the continuum of achievement. In Figure 8.1 the two continua of support are represented together. In the figure the two triangles that overlap represent the relations of the type/intensity and the setting of provision of support.

Even though in a schematic way Figure 8.1 presents a neat picture, the reality of education systems and schools is much more complex when referring to students receiving additional support. First, when referring to support *over and above* that which is available to 'all' students, some commentators, policy-makers and school personnel argue that the support triangle is a reverse one. This means that the 'larger' part of the base of the triangle, that is, a significant proportion of available support, is allocated to a small number of students (Figure 8.2). Secondly, and this relates again to the reverse continuum of support, there is an increase in the number of students requiring additional support across all levels of the triangle. Thirdly, the increased proportion of investment required by schools and teachers in providing additional support to a section of the school population affects the overall working of schools.

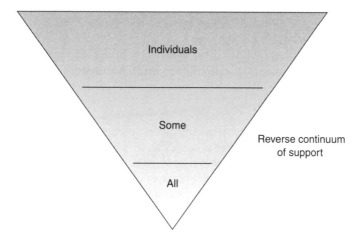

Figure 8.2   Reverse continuum of support

However, the extent to which the allocation of a large proportion of support is given to a small number of students may be seen as an issue of concern. Yet, if it is acknowledged that different students require different types and levels of support to participate and benefit from an educational experience, then providing this support, even when it is substantially different from that which other students receive, should not be an issue of concern in principle.

Nevertheless it is an issue of concern for a number of reasons. A prominent reason is that even though support is provided to groups and individual students, their educational outcomes are not in line with the continuum of achievement. In a crude way, the argument goes; some students despite the amount of support, effort and time invested in them do not perform to a level or in a way that is comparable with that of other students. According to the OECD (2003), recognizing the rights of students with diverse needs requires the provision of educational systems that are equitable for all and it is this concern with equity that should underline the provision of additional support. This same OECD report argues that the understanding of equity informing much educational policy is heavily influenced by Rawls's *Theory of Justice*.

Rawls's theory proposes a conception of justice that requires the unequal distribution of resources through society's institutions in order to benefit the least advantaged members of society. The difference principle that informs this conception of justice, is according to Rawls, 'a strongly egalitarian conception in the sense that unless there is a distribution that makes both persons better off (limiting ourselves to the two-person case for simplicity), an equal distribution is to be preferred' (Rawls, 1999: 66). Rawls's theory influenced positive discrimination initiatives in the latter part of the twentieth century. The concept of 'adjustment' as found in disability anti-discrimination legislation echoes Rawls's principle of difference.

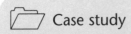 Case study

An example of anti-discrimination disability legislation

The *Australian Disability Standards for Education* (Australian Commonwealth, 2005) provide a framework for the implementation of the *Disability Discrimination Act* (Australian Commonwealth, 1992) in education. The Standards are the result of a consultation process involving stakeholders and aiming in achieving consensus decisions. In the case of education the development of the Standards has been lengthy while the development of standards in other areas, such as employment, was abandoned (Beecher, 2005). The *Disability Standards for Education* (2005) define an adjustment as a measure or action that is taken to assist a student with a disability to participate 'on the same bases as a student without a disability'. An adjustment is required because of the disability of the student. An adjustment is defined as reasonable 'if it balances the interests of all parties affected' (ibid.: 14). Thus if an adjustment benefits the disabled student but has not had an adverse effect the other parties involved (for example, the other students in the class, the staff or the education provider), then it may not be considered as reasonable.

Further, there is the question of the level of investment that is justifiable. In the case of the *Australian Disability Discrimination Act*, the concept of 'unjustifiable hardship' is used when an adjustment is considered reasonable but at the same time it causes a substantial burden, financially or in terms of resources to an education provider, that is, a school or education system.

In political philosophy there is a growing body of work that examines the position of disabled people as a 'hard case' or 'outliers' when deciding the arrangements of a just society. The starting point of this discussion is that social contract theory which is based on a process of bargaining for mutual advantage 'is so flawed that it cannot do justice to persons with disabilities' (Silvers and Francis, 2005: 41). This limitation was recognized also by Rawls. Building on Sen's capability approach, Nussbaum (2006) argues that in the capability approach, which is grounded in the language of human rights, core human entitlements that are seen as a bare minimum of what respect for human dignity requires must be detailed. For each capability there is a 'threshold level' that defines 'truly human functioning' for citizens and therefore social arrangements need to allow for citizens to be able to get above this capability threshold. In some ways the capability approach aims to provide a way to balance the continuum of achievement (in terms of individual outcomes that allow for functioning above the capability threshold) and the support required for this to happen.

According to Nussbaum (2006: 98–9): 'A satisfactory account of human justice requires recognizing the equal citizenship of people with impairments ... and appropriately supporting the labor of caring for and educating them ... It also requires recognizing ... the very great continuity between "normal" lives and those of people with lifelong impairments.' Although, Nussbaum's conception of impairment and disability understands these conditions or experiences as part of what may be termed normal human experience, she nonetheless draws a distinction between 'normal' lives and the lives of people with severe physical and intellectual impairments. This leads her to support the continuation of segregated and specialized provision for some disabled children and young people, and brings into question the possibility of a capability approach leading to significant advancement towards inclusive education and more broadly towards an inclusive society.

Terzi (2005: 454) also uses the capability approach to redefine impairment and disability and she argues that in education disability is a 'restriction in functioning achievements ... which relates to the design of educational system' and since the role of education is to expand capabilities then 'a child's limitations in functioning result in a restriction of the child's future capabilities'. In that sense disability is a vertical inequality or difference that needs to be addressed as a matter of justice. Thus, differential resources are understood in terms of equality rather than of assistance. The capability approach in terms of disability and education for the most part focuses on the response of education to impairment and disability and it does not pay attention to the potential of education to contribute or construct special education needs.

However, the relation between the individual right to education and the common good for a society that invests in an educational system is central to understanding how 'achievement' (in terms of educational outcomes) for individuals and schools is defined. To give an example of how this is translated in the articulation and justification of policy, in the Foreword of the *Excellence for All Children* (1997) the then Secretary of State for Education and Employment David Blunkett stated that:

> *The great majority* of children with SEN will, as adults, contribute economically; *all* will contribute as members in society. Schools have to prepare all children for these roles. That is a strong reason for educating children with SEN, *as far as possible*, with their peers. Where all children are included as *equal partners* in the school community, the benefits are felt by *all*. That is why we are committed to comprehensive and enforceable civil rights for disabled people. *Our aspiration as a nation must be for all our people*. (DfEE, 1997b: 4, emphasis added)

In the above extract, participation in society and productivity are separated, by acknowledging that a small proportion of children with special educational needs potentially are not going to be economically productive, without this negating their social role in society. Abberley (1996: 74) argues that the work-based model of social membership and identity can allow for the integration of a large proportion of the impaired population in the social work process but this is feasible to the extent that 'the interface between the individual's impairment, technology and socially valued activity produced a positive outcome'.

The acknowledgement of different contributions by disabled people to society (including but extending beyond employment) is of importance. However, achievement in different spheres of outcomes is ranked differently in education (and in society), with academic achievement being perceived and assessed as being of higher significance. Hence, the relation of the continua of achievement and support brings to the fore questions about the purpose of inclusive education, especially since 'for many disabled students, for example, no amount of resources could produce outcomes equal to those of their non-disabled peers' (OECD, 2003: 10). The investment required for the inclusion of disabled students in education cannot be seen as separate from dominant understandings of achievement in terms of desirable outcomes.

The successes and failures of inclusion

Very often a question asked is 'have educational systems become more inclusive?' This question can be asked at an international, regional, national, local, school and individual level. When we try to respond to this question the relation between the continuum of achievement and support is helpful in guiding our discussion. It is essential to see these continua as not limited to individual students or groups of students but rather as extending to the whole system.

At an international level it can be argued that many educational systems are now more inclusive than they were in the past when considering inclusion in terms of *entitlement*. For example, in numerous educational systems there is legislation that recognizes that disabled students have the right to education. In many educational systems where provision for disabled students was not available or was very limited and provided mainly by non-government organizations, there is an acknowledgement that the educational system (state, private or otherwise) needs to ensure that appropriate provision is available for disabled students. In a number of countries there is legislation or policy that recognizes that mainstream or general classrooms and schools should be an available option for disabled students. Further in a number of educational systems the general classroom or school is defined as the preferable first option for disabled students. These are very significant developments in the area of inclusive education, especially in cases where the entitlement to education for disabled students and students with special education needs reaffirms that all students, despite their individual characteristics, should have access to an education that is appropriate and relevant, that is, when educational systems respond, at least at the level of stated policy, to a broad definition of inclusion.

However, the actual effect of this development can be criticized in a number of ways as we have discussed throughout this book. Despite these developments, there is not an education system where we find that all students are educated in one type of school. Educational systems either operate segregated, specialized provision for part of the population of disabled students or in many countries a large proportion of disabled students do not participate in any type of education. In addition, processes and practices within regular schools allow for the allocation of students into 'streams', 'tracks', 'sets', and so on in terms of performance which may function as 'special classes' without the official label of 'special class'. The difficulty of collecting reliable statistical information and the differences in categories used across countries make it difficult to have a clear picture of whether there is actually a change in the proportion of students educated at different parts of the continuum of setting provision.

Further, there is evidence that increasing numbers of students are being identified as having 'special education needs' in many systems. Whether this is due to increased awareness, improved identification and assessment procedures, and the introduction of legislation that provides support, or is a result of schools trying to manage through special education practices students that do not 'fit' in terms of their academic and/or behaviour performance is a contested issue.

Finally, there is no clear picture about whether the outcomes of students identified as having special education needs or as receiving additional support have improved through policies that promote inclusion. The discussion, in Chapter 7, of the English context gives an indication of the complexity when trying to explore these issues.

For many writers, inclusion has been seen as a reform programme that is centred at the school level. Lipsky and Gartner (1997), working in the USA context, identify three waves of reforms that followed the publication of *A Nation at Risk* report. The first wave focused on external factors, the second wave on the role of adults while the third wave, which is the one that they propose, need to focus 'on a restructured and inclusive education system that serves well all students in a unitary fashion' (Lipsky and Gartner, 1997: 235). This reform requires a 'paradigmatic shift in education' based on 'a strength-based design, active learning, moving from student to life-long learner, striving for success from the start, parents and community as partners, new roles for school adults, and viewing differences as strengths' (ibid.: 235–6). However, this paradigmatic shift has not been realized.

It is clearly the case that many schools around the world have engaged with inclusion as a school reform project. Schools have tried to readdress notions of difference and diversity, outcomes and achievement and support. There is not a blueprint for this process but there are some characteristics that appear to facilitate greater success. For example, Giangreco (1997) refers to collaborative teamwork, a shared framework, family involvement, general educator ownership, clear roles for special educators, effective use of support staff, facilitating support services, and procedures for evaluating effectiveness.

The implementation of inclusion as a practice to be contested within the continua of achievement and support as described above, perpetuates what Minow (1985: 157) calls dilemma of difference; the question of how 'schools can deal with children defined as "different" without stigmatizing them on that basis'. Norwich (2008: 217) builds on this notion and develops a dilemmatic approach to inclusion identifying the identification, the curriculum, and the location dilemmas. For Norwich, a dilemmatic approach recognizes tensions and conflicts and 'involves accepting some crucial losses'. This is one example of what can be called a pragmatic approach to the implementation of inclusion at the school level. Schools are called to negotiate the complexities of the continua of achievement and support as imposed on the school externally and through the optimum use of available resources (support). Successful schools are those that can accommodate a high degree of 'diversity' (in comparison to other schools) and improve their performance (in relation to external indicators).

Although the literature in the area of school reform in inclusive education provides valuable insight into how schools can engage with practices that increase participation, the concept of an 'effective inclusive school' needs to be problematized. The 'effective inclusive school' is presented as typical and at the same time an atypical school. Inclusive practice at the school level is not something that each and every school is engaging with, but rather a practice that some schools have managed to develop when the right combination of circumstances exist, for example leadership that values and supports inclusion. This becomes more pertinent when the sustainability of inclusion is dependent on the continuation of those circumstances. The question of whether schools can sustain their engagement and success with inclusion (especially when it is linked to the external measures of achievement) highlights the precautious nature of this process.

Of interest is the work of Corbett (2001) which uses an ethnographic study in a school to describe a model of pedagogy that is based on three stages of differentiation. The three stages are presented in a reverse triangle where at the tip of the triangle there is an individual model (more traditional SEN approach), followed by an inclusive learning model (differentiated provision of learning tasks responding to learning styles) and by a valuing difference and empowerment model (wide range of pedagogies, valuing difference). This example of school-level practice focuses more on the pedagogies and practices utilized rather than the structural and organizational characteristics of an inclusive school.

In general, limited research into inclusive educational practice challenges curriculum arrangements and content. In fact, it can be argued that inclusive education has not engaged sufficiently with mainstream curriculum and it focuses mainly on how pedagogy can be differentiated for students who are experiencing difficulties so that they can access the mainstream curriculum. The uneasiness that characterizes the coexistence of inclusion/special education is even more evident in terms of instructive practices and strategies. However, existing research in this area shows that what works with students identified with special education needs works with all students.

A commitment to inclusive education for all students and a commitment to a common school open to all, providing the necessary support for meaningful learning and success, is not equated with the suggestion that everything that happens in general classrooms and schools is good or inclusive practice.

In this chapter we have used the principle of differentiation to discuss inclusion as it becomes policy and practice in schools. The continua of achievement and support guided our discussion at it was argued that a three-tiered system of support is neither inclusive nor exclusive. The use of the differentiation principle, to manage or remove individuals or groups that disrupt the smooth operation of the school, and the assumptions underpinning decisions about the cut-off points of providing support, within/without the regular classroom, limit the possibility of inclusion. In that sense asking the question of whether inclusion is successful is problematic since the success of inclusion is necessarily partial. In the same way, the failure of inclusion is partial.

For each account of schools embracing diversity and inclusion, there are more of schools that struggle or fail outright to engage with inclusion; for each teacher that effectively differentiates their curriculum and teaching practices to engage all learners, there are others that do not know how to begin this process from an inclusive perspective or who believe that it is not their job to do so; for each student that is welcomed in a classroom, there are others that are seen as problems to be got rid off; for each student that gets the additional support they need, there are others that do not.

Inclusive education faces a twofold issue to which it needs to respond: first that of the justification of inclusive practice and second that of how best to implement an inclusive education for all. The different theoretical frameworks used to justify inclusion – human rights, social model of disability, politics of difference, capabilities approach, and so on – propose different ways forward for education systems. However, most of the actual practice that is called inclusion falls short in realizing substantial change in the inclusive potential of educational systems and schools as well as the everyday experiences of students and teachers. One aspect of this failure is the fact that liberal education policy is committed to social reform rather than social transformation.

One of the complexities that inclusive education is faced with is that educational systems and schools do not simply need to balance what is offered and how it is offered to all students in order to balance support and outcomes (achievement). As we have discussed throughout this book, it is not simply that education systems do not provide the additional support and resources for the equitable participation of some groups, but also educational systems are structured in ways that create or reproduce inequalities. And, in fact, some of these inequalities operate through normalizing specific behaviours or ways of learning, or ways of being as innate 'problems' of the individual, through the discourse of 'needs'. The same school that removes barriers or provides additional support to facilitate the participation of some students adhering to existing anti-discrimination disability may operate in other ways that create student identities that lead to exclusion. Managing 'difference' in schools in relation to achievement requirements is a powerful driver in this process.

In an ethnographic study in a primary school on the effects of the *No Child Left Behind Act* (NCLB) in the USA, Harvey-Koelpin (2006) interviewed teachers in an urban school identified as failing under the NCLB. One of the teachers interviewed commented on teachers' willingness to accept students with special needs in their classrooms:

> Absolutely! Teachers don't want them. If my job depends on their test scores and they are reading at a first- or second-grade level and I am teaching fourth grade ... I don't want those kids. I do because I am a teacher and went into teaching to help kids. But if my job depends on it ... my car payments depend on it ... my apartment payment depends on it ... I don't want those kids. (Harvey-Koelpin, 2006: 140)

Resistance to inclusion remains a powerful factor in limiting educational transformation. Yet, resistance to inclusion, especially from teachers, teachers' unions, special education and disability organizations run by parents of disabled children, however, has perhaps changed focus. The initial resistance to inclusion as 'difficult' or 'utopian' has been replaced by the view that inclusive education was tried and failed and, even worse, was misguided from the start (Warnock, 2005).

While for many the main aim of inclusion's response should be to prove that it can work, we argue that it is the relation between difference and the purpose of education for individuals and the common good that needs to be redefined as part of the justification of the necessity for inclusion.

Summary

This chapter explored issues of policy and practice through the critical lenses of the principle of differentiation. This principle was used to discuss how what is considered as standard or universal practice in education is inevitably characterized by some type or degree of differentiation that creates tensions between the individual and common 'good'. These tensions were explored in relation to the two continua of achievement and support. In much of the literature of inclusive education the tension between the efficiency of an educational system in terms of outcomes (continuum of achievement) and equality in terms of provision of additional support (continuum of support) is seen as a 'balancing act'; this leads to what can be called a pragmatic approach to inclusive education.

There have been gains for inclusion in terms of anti-discrimination legislation, legislation promoting 'inclusion', and school reform. Although these gains are significant and in the long term establish an inclusive 'predisposition' within systems – an in principle commitment to inclusion – they do not challenge the fundamental tensions of the two continua. It is the enactment of the differentiation principle through an 'individual' model, if not a 'deficit' one, that continues to shape the 'inclusion problem' as a 'personal problem' (instead of a system problem). In that sense, the call for inclusion is perpetuated as utopian while the practice of inclusion is open to interpretations that water it down or distort it.

Thus, as we argued, inclusion as a radical project has not been implemented and therefore the claim that it has failed is unsubstantiated. The increasing resistance to inclusion cannot be counteracted by simply 'proving' that inclusion can work within the existing constrains of educational systems, but rather by re-radicalizing the inclusion project as an education imperative.

Discussion questions

- In what ways are inclusive policy and practice related?
- How is entitlement to participation and education defined?
- What models of provision at the system and school level can be defined as inclusive?
- What constitutes inclusive practice?
- Are there any schools that are inclusive?
- Can inclusion be sustained?

Further reading 📖

Brantlinger, E. (ed.) (2006) *Who Benefits from Special Education? Remediating (Fixing) Other People's Children*. Mahwah, NJ: Lawrence Erlbaum Associates.

Corbett, J. (2001) *Supporting Inclusive Education: A Connective Pedagogy*. London: Taylor & Francis.

Sindelar, P.T., Shearer, D.K., Yendol-Hoppey, D. and Liebert T. W. (2006) 'The sustainability of inclusive school reform', *Exceptional Children*, 72(3): 317–31.

Terzi, L. (2005) 'Beyond the dilemma of difference. The capability approach to disability and special educational needs', *Journal of Philosophy of Education*, 39(3): 443–59.

9

Exporting Inclusion to the Developing World

Chapter overview

Even with improved technology and communication, there is often still a considerable time lag between what occurs in the developed countries of the world and the developing world. When the concept of inclusion spread to developing countries, the definition was incongruous with the prevailing situation because the structure and conditions of societies in the South are different from those found in the countries of the North where the concept had been applied originally. Historically, the countries of the South were mostly colonies of the countries of the North with quite different internal political histories and social relations.

In the countries of the South there are usually greater budgetary constraints, less comprehensive education support and health-care systems, higher levels of unemployment, lower state contributions to welfare systems and minimal recognition of the rights of disabled people and other marginalized groups. These are usually the legacy of post-colonialism and we need to consider how inclusive educational thinking is effected in these former colonized countries. Moreover, what relevance do first-world models of practice have for the educational systems of developing countries where those countries often continue to play a service role for the economies of rich nations? This chapter explores the way models of inclusive educational practice developed in the first world have been exported as recipes to improve schooling as part of the international drive towards Education for All. The chapter considers the role of models and practices, commonly seen in the first world as empowering, such as the 'Index for Inclusion', from the critical perspective of a post-colonial analysis. It will also discuss some of the practical issues facing the developing world in maximizing opportunities for promoting inclusive education.

The *Salamanca Statement* calls on the international community to endorse the concept of inclusion within the education system and specifically looks to organizations like UNESCO, UNICEF, UNDP and the IBRD for support. This is presented as an issue of principle in respect of the human rights of children and young people. As Dessent (1987: 97) has argued

> Special schools do not have a right to exist. They exist because of the limitations of ordinary schools in providing for the full range of abilities and disabilities amongst children. It is not primarily a question of the quality or adequacy of what is offered in a special school. Even a superbly well organised special school offering the highest quality curriculum and educational input to its children has no right to exist if that same education can be provided in a mainstream school.

However, other considerations may have an equal if not greater bearing upon policy formulation and implementation in practice. For example, the UN *Standard Rules on the Equalization of Opportunities for Persons with Disabilities* (1993: Rule 6 of 22) recognizes that special schools may have to be considered where ordinary schools have not been able to make adequate provisions. By contrast, the World Bank, which works in conjunction with the United Nations to provide loans to developing countries, has argued in favour of inclusion, justifying this position primarily on the basis of the high cost of providing special schools for all children with special educational needs. If segregated special education is to be provided for all children with special educational needs, the cost will be enormous and prohibitive for all developing countries. Integrated in-class provision with a support teacher system is seen as a cheaper and more efficient alternative involving marginal costs.

Integration was the term made popular in Europe and North America in the 1970s. It involves the physical placement of learners in mainstream schools and the expectation that they will assimilate into the mainstream culture. Inclusion goes beyond integration and is concerned with a much more systematic adaptation and restructuring of mainstream schools to accommodate and respond to the diverse needs of their students. Yet, as we have indicated throughout this book, inclusive education is a very ambiguous concept and can be interpreted in various ways depending on the perspective of those proposing different positions. These include theoretical differences over the meaning of inclusion as well as (and following from) differences in policy and practice applications of the concept. As Barton (1997: 232) observed, these difficulties 'involve not merely semantic but also ideological and political issues'. Inclusion should perhaps also be understood as a dynamic and therefore unending process, rather than particular policies and practices being intrinsically inclusive or not. This would take account of the important contextual framing of history, together with social and cultural considerations.

The Index for Inclusion

How do we know that a school is moving towards inclusion? This is a difficult question to answer. One attempt to create a systematic tool for teachers to explore this question in the setting of their own school has been offered by the 'Index for Inclusion' developed by Tony Booth and Mel Ainscow in the UK. Inclusive education, according to Booth et al. (2002: 8) has three dimensions (creating inclusive cultures, producing inclusive policies and evolving inclusive practices). It is a tool that has been widely adopted by schools. In the UK the Index was distributed by that country's national Education Department to every mainstream and special school in England and Wales, so highly was its likely impact as a change agent considered to be. It is also an instrument that has been taken on board with some interest internationally, particularly in African and Latin American countries.

The Index is divided into four sections. Section 1 outlines an inclusive approach to school improvement and development. Section 2 offers guidance on a cyclical approach to inclusive school development. Section 3 provides a series of indicators that schools could use to reflect on any progress that has been made, and section 4 provides sample questionnaires for seeking views on various aspects of how inclusion is practised in schools and supported by the wider community.

The significance of the Index is that it adopts a systematic approach for the self-assessment of progress towards inclusion while allowing teachers themselves to specify their understanding of what inclusion means and the outcomes that will be used to evaluate progress towards their goals. The authors emphasize the value and opportunities for adapting it to local circumstances and conditions, and in many instances it clearly has been freely adapted for use in precisely the way intended. Creating inclusive cultures emphasizes the creation of 'a secure, accepting collaborating, stimulating community in which everyone is valued' (Booth et al. 2002: 8). Producing inclusive policies suggests that the concept of inclusion would be imbedded within the various school development plans and permeate all policies in an effort to 'increase the learning and participation of all students' (ibid.: 9). Philosophically driven inclusive cultures should guide the development of inclusive policies and should be reflected through inclusive practices. Therefore, inclusive practices are 'concerned with ensuring that classrooms and extra curricular activities encourage the participation of all students and draw on their knowledge and experience outside teaching. [It is expected that] teaching and support [be] integrated together in the orchestration of learning and the overcoming of barriers to learning and participation' (ibid.: 9). However, this approach can be seen as treating inclusive education in a somewhat formulaic fashion and there are, inevitably, risks and preconceptions that arise from any formulaic approach, no matter how flexible and adaptable the tool is. In particular, sufficient weight may not be given to differing interpretations of education across the world.

Education cannot be defined simply as schooling. The interrelationship of schools within a national system of education, the political and the policy frameworks of educational practice, the economic impacts on education, and the interrelationship of national educational systems and priorities within a framework of international power relations all add complexity to an understanding of inclusion within an educational discourse. So, too, do local historical, social and cultural traditions need to be considered. In this sense, educational issues cannot be construed simply as problems that can be solved at the school level through responsive forms of management. Such an approach would be akin to taking private industry practices that are supported by training schemes and 'how to' manuals, and aligning them to schools to promote well-being. Some would argue that such an approach would favour teacher and local managerial autonomy, thus promoting economy, efficiency and effectiveness, and the Index for Inclusion can easily, if unintentionally, lead policy-makers and managers to adopt this approach as a school improvement initiative.

Likewise the risks of cultural imperialism with a tool such as the Index are very real. Adaptable it may be, but it both provides a framework for thinking about school improvement that is imposed, and can be imposed very crudely (see the following case study) and may decontextualize school practice from wider socio-political and economic challenges and struggles. The nature of research and development collaborations between special educators from first-world countries and developing countries, especially where the former are acting as change-agents may take for granted concepts such as 'equity', 'social justice' and 'human rights'. They are represented as having universal meaning without influence from the specific historical and cultural traditions of developing countries. When introduced as guiding principles of education reform, these taken for granted ideas (developed in the Western philosophical and political traditions over many centuries) obfuscate the unequal relationships between countries and the dependency promoting outcomes of change-oriented development interventions. Thus, when policies on inclusive education are abstracted from the broader social context within which they are situated it is unlikely that they will be effective.

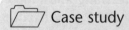 Case study

In a research study funded by the UK's Department for International Development a research team using the Index for Inclusion sought to engage in action research with schools in Kenya and Tanzania to enhance inclusion education practice. The English research team identified and trained facilitators in the two countries concerned. It was these facilitators who were responsible for working with local schools in the two countries. However, the facilitators, although experienced educators in the countries concerned, were not themselves local to the school districts involved in the intervention. The interventions had variable outcomes. One problem that the facilitators encountered was in engaging the voices of students. This was considered to be necessary, perhaps even axiomatical, if an insight into the nature and extent of inclusion within these schools was to be understood. This approach was resisted by the teachers, and students were reluctant to give their views. The researchers in the UK, in explaining this non-engagement and its implications, argued that it reflected the local culture in which a young person's voice was only allowed to be heard when they had gone through a rite of passage into adulthood. This was identified by the researchers as a problem to be overcome in the schools in becoming more inclusive.

The case study raises four questions for consideration:

1. What implications should be drawn from the clash between the local culture of 'voice' being earned through a rite of passage and the framing of inclusion by the research team in their intervention with these schools?
2. What were the advantages and disadvantages of using local (but not from that region or speakers of local languages) facilitators from the two countries in which the interventions took place?
3. How would you justify interventions like this led by a team of researchers from the developed world in countries of the developing world? What arguments could be made against such interventions?
4. How might a collaboration between developed world and developing world educators be constructed in ways that retain power and control in the hands of local educators?

Further questions for reflection

- How would the Index work in a situation where teachers have lower level secondary education and teach classes of 60 or more students and the numbers keep increasing in spite of the shortage of teachers?
- How would use of the Index support children of farming communities that fail economically because the prices of their crops have dropped in the international market in the free trade market?
- How can the Index support education in a system where children who go to school live in constant threat of HIV/AIDS, malaria and tuberculosis?
- How can the Index be used to allow people in the developing world to have a voice in local politics and the framing of the society in which they live?
- What might be considered appropriate education for communities who are constantly living on the edge?

Developing countries: perspectives and issues

A large percentage of children with special educational needs have been included in the public education systems of developing countries. Nonetheless, the goals of equity and equality of opportunity remain distant for the majority of people. Even where the average child has access to education this does not mean that those children receive an education appropriate to their needs. For example, those stricken by poverty often experience academic deceleration and acquire special educational needs as they pass through the school system, leading to their eventual exclusion from those sections of the school system that offer the greatest prospects for upward social mobility (UNESCO, 1996b). Unfortunately, the majority of theorists from the developed West apply Western theories to the entire world without due consideration of the economic situation, cultural heritage and composition, and without truly listening to the voices and experiences of those who have experienced colonization as part of their history and have day-to-day experience of the challenges of educational and economic development. As Connell (2007: 44) points out there is a 'northernness' to these theories where '[d]ebates among the colonized are ignored and intellectuals of the colonized societies are unreferenced, and social process is analysed in an ethnographic time warp'. There is an arrogance of interpretation where it is assumed that people from very different countries will either experience the world in the same way or that systems developed and working well in the developed world could be easily and successfully replicated in economically, culturally and politically different 'developing systems'.

Ten years after the 'Education for All' World Conference in Jomtien, representatives from the countries of the Americas (Latin America, the Caribbean and North America) met in February 2000 to assess the progress made thus far (UNESCO, 2000). Commitments were made at this meeting to advancing the cause of Education for All in 12 areas based on the premise that everyone had a right to 'high-quality basic education from birth'. These areas were: early childhood care and education; basic education; satisfying basic learning needs of young people and of adults; learning achievements and quality of education; inclusive education; education for life; increase of national investment in education and effective mobilization of resources on all levels; professional enhancement of teachers; new opportunities for participation of the community and the society; linking of basic education to strategies for overcoming poverty and inequity; utilization of technologies in education; and management of education.

The commitments were made in recognition that basic education for all requires genuine opportunities for access, permanence, quality learning, and full participation for all children and adolescents, including indigenous students, those with disabilities and those who are homeless or working, and so on. Education for All also implies protection for those from different ethnic language and social groups, as well as women. Moreover, respect for individual differences by education systems is essential.

Those countries represented at the conference pledged to formulate inclusive education policies that define goals and priorities in respect of those groups who were currently excluded from education within their countries. This entailed an explicit commitment to establishing appropriate legal and institutional frameworks, the design of diversified education delivery systems and flexible school curricula to support diverse needs; the strengthening of inter-cultural education; and, the implementation of a sustained process of communication for communities and families that emphasizes the importance and the benefits of educating those who are currently excluded (UNESCO, 2000).

But what is meant by these universalistic notions of inclusion? Do they really go anywhere beyond rhetoric? Since the introduction of the term 'inclusion', there has been a movement arguing for children with special needs to be included into 'regular' schools as advocated by the Salamanca Statement (1994).

 Point for reflection

What does 'regular' actually mean? Can we pause a moment and define a 'regular' school. Choose any regular school from any country on the planet and define the characteristics. What does it look like? Who does it cater to? What is the size of the school? Is it secular or religious based? What sort of amenities does it have or have access to? What are the characteristics of the teachers who work there? Does the idea of a 'regular' school not itself imply some form of defining what is 'normal' and, if it does, does this idea not lead to the exclusion or self-exclusion of some groups or individuals?

If we look at the concept of Education for All, it may be argued that the United Nations is proposing a system for all children without an understanding or appreciation that it may not be effective for all. Does *one* size really fit all children? Does not the idea impose a form of homogeneity (Wedell, 2005). Perhaps, we should be looking at ways to provide individual support for learners based on their needs in ways that allow them to achieve successes in a multiplicity of ways rather than using comparative measures of success. The focus might then be on achieving the maximum potential of the learner.

Point for reflection

Recently, one of our Indonesian students, Nur, shared these thoughts with us. She got the idea from a Singaporean publication entitled 'Suzuki Versus Porsche' published in 1997. We are all gifted. Because we are all individuals, some of us open our gifts earlier than others. Some of us are very quick-minded, speedy and flashy and we can perceive ourselves as sports cars, like the Porsche or the Maserati or the Aston Martin. Then, there are some of us who are not so quick and we may have dents and bruises and may not have a sleek aerodynamic exterior and may be likened to little vans and pick-ups – not so fast and far less flashy. But when we negotiate through the crowded streets of the town or the city centre we are all navigating an even playing field because there is a certain ethic that applies to all vehicles regardless of their brand. Neither the sports car nor the van or pick-up is given a special advantage to weave through the traffic. At that point, they have an equal chance of making it to their destination and that's the significant point. Each vehicle is going to their destination. In the final analysis, does it really matter who gets there first? The important thing is that we all arrive at our chosen destination confidently and honourably.

Throughout the learning process, all students regardless of their ability, their skin colour, their cultural heritage, their gender, their social class, the size of their parents' wallets should be able to negotiate a pathway in life, identify opportunities and at the same time also become aware of risks. They should learn how and when to use the various tools within their vehicles so that they could more effectively and efficiently move forward, apply the brakes, change the gear, turn in a different direction, and so on. Our students should learn that sometimes on the way to their destination, they may have to move faster, slow down, pull aside to rest, turn left or right or even make a 'U' turn.

- How can we now reconceptualize the role of the teacher within an inclusive classroom?
- How can we apply this analogy inclusively to the various teaching and learning situations in the world?

To see inclusive education as an end, rather than as a debate about the purposes of education, is to see it in two quite different ways. One of the great concerns that we have is about the way in which inclusive education is operating in the world today, in the absence of any serious critical analysis of what it is or of what inclusive education might even mean and its implications in different social contexts. What has been happening is that it is being exported into different contexts; and this is actually serving to manipulate or distort those contexts in ways which de-politicize some of the issues around education particularly in the developing world.

We do not believe that the countries of the North can produce models for the countries of the South because to do so would be highly inappropriate, patronizing and in fact represent one more post-colonial exertion of power. This does not mean they have nothing to offer. Both parties need to engage in greater dialogue with the people themselves, and ask them 'What do they want for their people/country/children? What do you hope to achieve in all of this?' Educators from the developed world need to appreciate that what others want or need may not be what would be expected by those from the developed world. Ideas that may seem appropriate based on one's own experience do not necessarily translate into something that is 'good for' people whose experience is quite different. This realization is about respecting other peoples, and it is not about fixing the world because we cannot fix it by transposing it into a first-world paradigm with a first-world understanding.

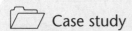 Case study

Yes they could and **they did**

About 20 years ago, a group of teachers in Trinidad were looking for support in the teaching learning process in special needs education. The government was spending a lot of money on contracting 'experts from the developed north' to provide workshops for their teachers. Unfortunately, upon completion of the workshops, teachers were told how excellent they were but no one was receiving genuine certification. After several discussions, the teachers got together and said 'Why are they spending all this money, and giving it to the outside region, to give us models that are not working? Why can't we become qualified ourselves, and get our own people to work with us in a way that we understand the world?' And that is exactly what happened. They knew the goal was one of internal empowerment, but they also needed a certificate with international currency. They approached a university in the UK to work with them to develop the curriculum in a way that honoured the wisdom of their senior special educators, the integrity of the people and the local traditions that were an important part of the local culture. The understanding was that they would only work with the university if there was a genuine respect for the personhood of the senior educators who were invited to become a very real part of the course management team. This programme has changed over time and it continues to contribute to the educational development of the people of the Caribbean. The programme continues to live and breathe through the many persons scattered across the globe who have benefited from it. If you want to support people from a particular region with a different culture, you have to start where they are at, and engage with them at that level in ways that they understand the world.

The need for collaboration between home and school can be nowhere more evident than in small economies. Here parents work long hours, earn meagre wages and may be away from home for extended periods. Parental involvement is critical to the changing of attitudes among communities. There is a past perception that the school took the place of the home for the student who lacked appropriate support at home. This notion requires closer examination in light of the fact that the role and status of teachers have changed. Teachers no longer see their role automatically as surrogate parents and, as a result, the expected support for students experiencing social, emotional, behavioural or learning difficulties in the system may not be present. Perhaps through the medium of parental and community involvement, parents can both monitor the performance of schools and have an opportunity to define the direction for this relationship. Parents and the wider community should be embraced as partners in education to break down some of the barriers that some teachers have erected to bar parents from participating in aspects of the education process and to reinforce the contribution of parents to support educational reform.

Developing a truly inclusive system begins with the recognition of the importance of early childhood care and education as a crucial area providing a foundation for future educational success. Around the world, various initiatives have being undertaken in response to this. For example, in some countries, pre-primary settings have been annexed to the primary school in an attempt to bring early childhood education in line with the mainstream system. However, responsibility for such initiatives varies considerably between developing countries. Moreover, despite recognition of the importance of early childhood education, priorities across the world nonetheless remain focused on the tertiary, secondary and primary levels, which are perceived to be more important areas demanding reform and interventions, not least because these are areas for which national governments at present have more direct responsibility.

The focus on appropriate pre-primary education can largely determine the extent to which individual territories can respond to the notion of 'education for all'. It is our experience that as evidence of training, support and proper monitoring of early childhood care and provision increased and improved, the general education systems showed a greater level of consciousness and response to the need for quality education. This, however, requires further training for providers to prepare them to support and work with *all* children in the system. The bottom line is that an adequate early childhood care and education (ECCE) system would include systems for early detection of educational difficulties and strategies for early intervention. This could be linked to a parenting programme where parents could be supported with proper parenting skills which would not be discriminatory in its practice. So important is early childhood care and education that the 2007 *EFA Global Monitoring Report* focuses on this particular goal and calls upon countries to improve and expand its support for our future leaders of the world (UNESCO, 2006).

 Point for reflection

In our schools, communities and other places of work how can we:

- promote inclusion?
- challenge prejudice and promote positive attitudes towards all people?
- use our positions as members of communities to show our respect for different cultural rights and perspectives?
- implement various types of policy to promote inclusion? Policy-makers make policy. People on the ground implement them. Policy is meaningless without practice.

Indigenous communities

In all the excitement surrounding the achievement of universal primary education and education for all, very little consideration is given to the effect of these aspirations on Indigenous communities with traditional knowledges. Very often traditional knowledges regarding health, education, governance and agriculture from various countries in Africa, the Caribbean and Australia, to name a few, are discounted by development specialists who believe that the current understanding that they possess in their areas of expertise is far superior to that held for centuries by traditional societies. This view of Indigenous cultures is easily reinforced when the major focus for development is placed on meeting such grand (rhetorical?) targets such as those emblazoned in the Millennium Development Goals (MDGs) and evaluated according to predetermined measurable Indicators which were crafted in a cultural vacuum without any meaningful reference point to the cultural norms, beliefs and understandings of Indigenous communities. The West has to recognize that there is relevance to local cultural knowledge and that this knowledge remains valuable in the twenty-first century. One such example is the Aboriginal tradition of using the land as conservation and renewal practice. Aboriginal rangers in Central Australia are now working with white Australian rangers to conserve the land and teach them the traditions that have preserved the land for over 40,000 years.

The international community assumes that because primary education has had such a positive effect on several communities around the world that it could just as easily be transferred to Africa with the same positive impact. One of the considerations here is the extent of the colonial legacy in terms of education, health, skill base and strength of economy. One has to recognize that reform systems which equate with 'quick fixes' will be unsuccessful in countries where there are deep-rooted challenges, especially if the reforms do not respectfully consider cultural norms, values and practices. Country systems whose colonial inheritance from France, England and Portugal could be described as nothing short of traumatic cannot simply be transformed as a result of international pronouncements and outside interventions. Africa is a particularly difficult continent because of the cycle of economic, health and knowledge poverty that exists in many of the countries as a result of the negative effects of colonialism, international loan conditionalities and resultant structural adjustments, HIV/AIDS and militarism. Unfortunately the challenges of low infant mortality, the lack of education for girls and women, access to clean water, food, medicines for common diseases, and effective family planning measures cannot simply be solved by the introduction of universal primary education. Though it can be viewed as a worthwhile endeavour, it cannot be viewed as a panacea for structural challenges. What is required is an ongoing engagement with local governments, principals, teachers and parents in a way that respects their cultural traditions and understanding of the world and moves them gently along the path of education.

If education is to be meaningful to people, it must be contextualized and learning should be initiated out of the very real experiences of the learner through dialogue which is developed around themes of significant importance to these learners. Learners have their own history and culture which impinge on their learning and so the voice of the learner must be situated within a historical and cultural context because it is moulded by their experiences. This should be the starting point for any educative process which seeks social transformation as its goal.

In order to achieve the goals of educational transformation, one needs to consider the use of dialogic culture circles. Dialogue encourages collaborative learning by limiting 'teacher-talk'. It allows people to name their experience and encourages them to find their voice within the context. Critical pedagogy is a term that has undergone several transformations as educators engage with issues that infiltrate teaching and learning that have their roots in history. Critical pedagogy looks at ways of deploying different strategies that explore education in a manner that is contextualized within its social and historical contexts. It seeks to throw a spotlight on education systems that have their roots in colonialism as with countries like India, Indonesia, Malaysia, the Philippines and Vietnam, as well as those in Africa, Latin America and the Caribbean.

This approach focuses on the liberation of the mind, the raising of critical consciousness and the reconfiguring of the traditional teacher/learner relationship where the teacher is the fountain of all knowledge. The classroom then becomes transformed because it is now a place of discovery, of possibilities, of personal growth, of exchange through dialogue and groundedness of both teachers and learners. In this approach, the focus is on liberatory education where the teacher supports the enabling of the learners to see themselves as powerful and meaningful in the learning context. The learners are guided into understanding the issues in a social context and to assist in the development of strategies for challenging these issues in a constructive manner that has a liberatory effect on the learners as they begin to experience success. Learners are then further empowered through 'praxis' where they are taught how to think about their learning, apply new strategies, evaluate the effectiveness of those strategies, reflect on the entire cycle and then repeat the cycle on an ongoing basis. Social transformation only becomes possible when 'praxis' is applied in an ongoing collective manner.

By viewing schools both as cultural sites as well as instructional institutions, we can begin to unpack our own practices, looking at ways in which we are overwhelmingly subjective and become more visionary to encourage critical learning, civic courage and active citizenship. In order for learning to be powerful and engaging in a meaningful and positive manner, one has to address the various contexts of the everyday lives of learners, looking at cultural relevance, artefacts, media, and so on, looking at ways in which meanings are represented and constructed and to move learning beyond those points of leverage.

Today, as educators we all face the challenges of educating people to eventually live in a very challenging world. These are indeed exciting times that we live in, with more development taking place than we have ever seen before in our evolution. Although as teachers, we may strive for a more liberatory approach to teaching, we need to acknowledge that inherent in our competence as pedagogues is the notion of authority. Freire has argued that this authority should never degenerate into authoritarianism and, if he was alive today, he would probably insist that this authority should rest on the strength of humility and love (Mayo, 1999). We would argue that authority should be translated into *responsibility for promoting the empowerment of others and respect for and the valuing of diversity and difference*. If, as educators, we require our students to become critically active citizens of the world, then we need to recognize the relationship between power and knowledge and to acknowledge that power lies in the guises of race, gender and class. This is part of our colonial heritage and it is not going to disappear unless we learn to unpack and deconstruct these labels and the attendant practices which support their perpetuation in a negative manner.

Teacher education and professional learning

The importance of professional learning and development should not be underestimated in promoting a broad understanding of inclusive education and policy and practice both within countries of the North and the South. Professional learning can only make a real impact when there ceases to be a separation between special education and general education, when education courses are totally integrated at all levels within the education system and special education is no longer seen as simply an add-on. Government and tertiary education policy should ensure that there is no longer a dichotomy between what has previously been described as regular and special education. Such education opportunities should provide spaces where teachers not only learn new and innovative strategies for teaching pupils with a wide range of differing abilities, but also those which promote the development of creativity so that teachers could develop strategies which promote active learning and can be adapted to individual needs.

Smith and Motivans (2007) argue that although there has been a growth in the number of students in sub-Saharan Africa, there has not been a proportionate increase in the number of teachers, resulting in an increase in the teacher:pupil ratio. For example, even though the median 2004 ratio was 46 pupils to 1 teacher, a closer investigation of the situation revealed that in Ethiopia the ration was 70:1 and in Chad, Congo, Malawi, Mozambique and Rwanda was in excess of 60:1. At the lower end of the scale Gambon, Senegal, Seychelles and Togo were below the median.

Reports from the majority of developing countries point to serious problems in respect of teacher education and pedagogy within the schools. While some teachers' colleges and universities are operating at a more advanced level than others in terms of the quality of the educational opportunities provided, the majority need a major rethinking of their teacher training strategy. Very often the teacher training strategy is not linked to any national education reform and the colleges and universities are entities which operate autonomously. As a result, teachers do not have the necessary training (skills and knowledge) to work with children who have special educational needs. For the most part, they experience difficulty working with those whom they label as 'slow learners' in the system. In China, teachers who have difficulty working with children who experience learning difficulties explain that it's 'difficult for children who are not clever to study.' (Heung and Grossman, 2007: 173). In Indonesia, there is often a mismatch between the lives of the children and the context of the school in terms of culture, language and focus. In funding the reform of their education systems governments needs to give serious consideration to what the reform would look like and what interventions would be meaningful from the perspective of the millions of students in that system. Would the curriculum as it stands serve them as they become adults in that society and how aligned is the curriculum to the national priorities? There need to be mechanisms which support teachers in transferring new knowledge to local situations, especially when they have been accustomed to teaching in systems which previously fostered rote learning.

In the countries in which we have worked it is not uncommon for teachers to believe that their training at the teachers' colleges did not adequately prepare them for teaching in the education system. The education that they receive is too theoretical and geared towards formal examinations rather than educational practice in the classroom. In many instances, the teaching practice component was not realistic and pedagogy was largely ignored. We think that it is very important to provide ongoing opportunities for the further upgrading of skills for teacher educators within the region. This would not only improve their skills but provide some measure of motivation.

A critical area of concern within developing countries is the promotion of outstanding teachers to administrative positions in the various Ministries of Education. In many instances these promoted teachers are assigned to senior positions, sometimes in totally new discipline areas without sufficient training to meet the demands of a new position. This may not always produce the desired effect. As a result, there may be little benefit to the system through such decision. Persons should be promoted based on training and ability, not on length of service. If teachers are to be promoted within the education system, they should be appropriately trained before they are appointed to their next level of service.

Greater focus should also be given to the teaching of research skills. There needs to be recognition that research creates education, and opportunities should be made available for those in the education system to be engaged in practical research within their countries and regions. During this period where there is much data collection as a result of the worldwide focus on EFA and the delivery of the MDGs, there is a greater opportunity to develop these research skills through linkages between government Ministries of Education, universities and colleges. Yet, there remains a lack of consistency in this area. More often than not government ministries have not given research either the priority or the resources that are required if it is to make a serious and useful contribution to educational planning and development.

Universities, for their part, often treat research as something that is extremely difficult which can only be done by someone with higher postgraduate qualifications. Action research undertaken by teachers, in particular, is often treated disparagingly and not supported in ways that could enhance its validity and relevance. Moreover, the absence of university and college campuses in some of the developing countries places these countries at a serious disadvantage, both in terms of 'higher education' support for the development of regional strategies and in terms of the accessibility of skilled personnel to work with teachers and schools.

Some universities and countries have invested heavily in distance learning technologies to support advanced professional qualifications for teachers but problems with pedagogy cannot be adequately addressed using a remote, distance learning mode of delivery. Face-to-face sessions and the modelling of good pedagogical practice are needed to support effectively distance learning modes of intervention in teacher education. Teachers will learn by doing. Appropriate pedagogies for classroom teaching cannot be taught via computer screens or by books and other written materials alone.

Our view is that professional education has to be more open to an engagement with new thinking about curriculum and pedagogy and research, joining in the international debates around those areas and exploring issues for collaboration and international exchange. Professional learning can be used to keep teachers and those within the education system abreast of important developments in policy and practice that occur internationally, regionally and nationally. Teachers can workshop different ways of developing the curriculum so that they support broad development goals in ways that are culturally relevant and economically feasible while being able to support the diverse needs of the learners. Professional learning should also be mandatory for all education administrators whose short-sightedness or ignorance could obstruct any reform rather than promote or facilitate progress.

In spite of these proposed changes, it must be recognized that one cannot suggest changes in the type and nature of professional learning and teacher education programmes without changes in government policies and general conditions of work. If world governments are serious about Education for All and the achievement of the MDGs, then consideration must be given for the support of education systems of the world where there could be provision made for classroom resources, appropriate class sizes and para-professional support where necessary.

Summary

Very often as we travel along our busy roads of life, we forget about the importance of laying a solid foundation for the future leaders of tomorrow. We cannot afford to forget that if we are to provide appropriate support for our children so that they can *all* experience a sense of well-being, inclusion should begin from the cradle with protection for their mothers, the delivery of appropriate health care and adequate nourishment. Quality education at all levels needs to be flexible, relevant and interesting to the society that it serves. We cannot continue to force Northern models on Southern spaces.

Further reading 📖

Booth, T. and Ainscow, M. (2002) *Index for Inclusion. Developing Learning and Participation in Schools.* Bristol: CSIE Ltd.

Connell, R. (2007) *Southern Theory: The Global Dynamics of Knowledge in Social Science.* Sydney: Allen & Unwin.

Sen, A. (2003) 'The importance of basic education' *EducationGuardian.co.uk*, 28 October. Available from: http://people.cis.ksu.edu/~ab/Miscellany/basiced.html

UNESCO (2006) *EFA Global Monitoring Report 2007. Strong Foundations: Early Childhood Care and Education.* Paris: UNESCO. Available from: www.unesco.org/en/efareport/reports/2007-early-childhood/ (accessed on 20 April 2009).

Section 4

Conclusions and Reflections

In this final section of the book we draw together the key themes that have been developed throughout the book and sketch out ideas for rethinking the inclusive education project framed by the broader relationships between the contested values of education and the practical possibilities for making a difference. Finally we share some of our own personal perspectives on our individual and collective journeys, and offer an invitation to join us in this process of critically engaging with a crucial issue in educational theory, policy and practice.

10

A Conclusion or a Starting Point for the Future?

> ## Chapter overview
>
> We have argued that the inclusive education movement in theory, policy and practice has in many respects been an illusion. Yet that is not the whole story because it is also a struggle for change, a struggle for justice and fairness, and a struggle for the value and valuing of human life. Educational policy and practice are highly contested in different local contexts and it is in these contextualized struggles over the values and purposes of education that hope lies. We draw together the main themes of this book and sketch out some ideas for rethinking the inclusive education project framed by the broader relationships between the contested values of education and the practical possibilities for making a difference.

In this book we have looked at the idea of inclusive education from a number of different perspectives: from philosophical and historical perspectives; from the perspective of policy; and, from the perspective of practice. Our reach in the discussion has had a wide compass because we believe that the idea of inclusion is not relevant just for particular groups and individuals, who are seen as excluded from the mainstream of schools or society. It has also been global. We have examined several international initiatives and policies, including the goals of *Education for All* (1990) and the *Millennium Declaration* (2000), the *Salamanca Statement* (1994), the *World Declaration on Human Rights* (1948), and the UN Rights of the Child. In fact these are all frameworks for action rather than binding policies. However, of the 192 member countries of the United Nations who have expressed commitment to the concept of Education for All, more than 80 per cent of the countries of the North and more than 50 per cent of the countries of the South do in fact have written policies on inclusive education. Yet, these governments have all interpreted inclusion differently. In practice we find that inclusion policies may not include the gypsies of Eastern Europe or the Indigenous peoples of the USA, Australia, Dominica or Guyana, or the millions of war refugees scattered around the globe or the poor people who become nomads in their search for jobs and a sense of belonging for themselves and their families. These contradictions in themselves suggest that policies on inclusive education may not be written, stated, understood or enacted in similar ways. In addition, we should remember that what education technocrats, bureaucrats and teachers enact as policy may differ in key respects from the written or official documents which articulate both national policies and international proclamations.

We have argued that the term inclusive education has in many respects become synonymous with special education, that is, with approaches to education that treat the disabled or disruptive child as different from the 'normal' child and in need of special treatment or intervention, mostly directed towards an identified individual 'need'. The idea of inclusive education was grounded in a critique of education and of broader social systems which themselves were seen to be disabling of, or discriminatory towards, people by putting them into categories outside the mainstream. Moreover, a review of the world situation, suggests that the definition of inclusive education must be broadened to address not only the needs of those who have been placed within the different classifications of special educational needs but also those who are disenfranchised as a result of poverty, ethnic or gender discrimination, or for various other reasons. The *Final Report of the World Conference on Special Education – Access and Quality* (1994: 15) offers the following very broad definition that does encompass this view:

> The concept of special educational needs will also include, besides disabled people, all those who are experiencing difficulty on a temporary or permanent basis, who are repeating continually their school years, who are forced to work, who live on the streets, who live far from any school, who are extremely poor, who are victims of wars, who suffer abuses, or who are simply out of school, for whatever reason.

This definition reminds us that if people are denied education or the opportunity to learn new things that equip them for life within their community, it is this lack of opportunity that is disabling because their potential is being limited when we propose and support systems that are riddled with inequalities.

In the book we have explored three central areas:

- The history of inclusive education.
- The development of policy both in the countries of the North and the South.
- The translation of policy into practice.

We have argued that in its origins inclusive education was inextricably linked to debates about the role of special education. The expansion of systems of special education was a direct outcome of the industrialization of production in the North in the nineteenth century. This created a dual need: on the one hand the need for a manual labour force with basic educational competencies and compliance and, on the other, the need for a way of managing those children who failed to accept the principle of authority within the industrial mass education system and those who were seen as unable to contribute in due course to the workforce. Special education quickly became a safety valve for the mainstream school.

In creating a special education system some spaces were opened up for enhancing the quality of educational experience and life opportunities for those who were excluded from the mainstream. In time, and particularly, in the context of changes within the mainstream education system and wider social and economic changes in society, contradictions within traditional approaches to both mainstream education and special education gave rise to new thinking about inclusive education. This focused in part upon the rights of all children to have access to genuine educational opportunities as participating citizens whatever the nature or degree of their impairment.

The development of inclusive education policy and practice, however, has been beset by problems relating to what the concept really means. We have maintained that this is not simply an argument about definitions, although there are many competing and conflicting definitions. Rather we suggest that it reflects differences of perspective and intent grounded in material realities concerning the purpose of education in society. In other words, the problem of definition is a political problem. This understanding is reinforced by the thinking about inclusive education that has informed debates about educational entitlement and national development in the developing countries of the South.

Inclusive education policy-making has reflected these differences of perspective. We have explored this in three different settings. The first of these was centred upon the United Nations policy agencies and the international development funding agencies. We have examined how thinking about inclusion has been influenced by the development needs (including the history of colonial domination and economic exclusion) of the countries of the South and constrained by the policy (and political) priorities of international funding agencies; the latter sometimes in conflict between different agencies.

In Europe, the rhetoric around inclusion has reflected the widespread concern by governments about ways of managing the social impacts of the rapidly expanding European Union. Yet, the rhetoric masks continuing policy fragmentation across Europe and national differences abound. Looking at policy development in England we saw clear evidence of the strong rhetoric of inclusion in the reform of national educational policy over the last decade. Nonetheless, we have argued that this rhetoric is framed by priorities around school improvement and educational efficiency within the mainstream sector which are not necessarily aligned with a human rights or entitlement perspective on inclusion.

In the third section of the book we have looked at future directions in inclusive education and in particular at issues arising from the translation of inclusive education theories and policies into practice. The key issue continues to centre on the purpose of schooling. We argue that where the management of difference is the focus of interventions this inevitably leads to the reconstruction of the ideology of separate systems of special education, even if under a different name. Our focus in these chapters, therefore, is on understanding and ways of changing educational philosophy and practice within the education sector as a whole and in the mainstream school in particular.

The continuing conflicts over the purpose of education are illustrated by the ways in which educators from the North in working in countries of the South engage with issues of inclusive education. We have raised serious concerns about models of the educational expert decontextualized from the real lives of students, teachers and their schools and communities. Even when interventions of this sort reflect genuine humanitarian attempts to assist in educational transformation they are fraught with difficulties and in danger of being idealistic and ill-founded. By imposing values and solutions that reinforce the domination of the North, they easily demonstrate the continuing relevance of Freire's critique of the 'culture of silence'. It is a silence produced by a history of oppression and an outcome of the intellectual and cultural dominance of the North over the South. Its impact is still felt in today's world as the result of the cultural and economic capital accumulated in the North through those unequal relations.

Inclusive education presents us with many challenges. Who can be against the idea of inclusion? Yet we have seen that the reality is far more complex. There are lessons to learn. These include the need to understand the politics of inclusion and the histories within which systems of education have developed and been contested over time, and they include the importance of understanding and improving our approaches towards collaboration and genuine partnership, be it with people from across different sections of our own societies or between societies with very different but nonetheless interconnected histories. More than anything, the idea of inclusive education stands out for hope and a belief in the possibility of fair and just relationships between people. Even as an ideal, recognizing the importance of a critical engagement with this idea, it is, we believe, an ideal that is worth the struggle.

An Epilogue on Reflection

Positioning ourselves in the field of inclusive education

We have each travelled our separate journeys and have each come to inclusive education in a different way. In this final reflection each of us shares with you some reflections on our personal journeys so that perhaps you too can dare to reflect on yours.

Ann Cheryl's journey

I see education as a political issue and my involvement with and understanding of special education and inclusion are intimately linked to my political journey from 1985 to now.

During the period 1981–84, the University of Manitoba in conjunction with the Government of Trinidad and Tobago conducted four professional development projects aimed at improving the teaching strategies of teachers working with children with special educational needs. These were funded by the Canadian International Development Agency (CIDA) and the workshops attracted approximately 1,100 teachers, which was approximately one-tenth of the country's teachers from mainstream schools. Many of the participants only had a general understanding of pedagogy being 'diplomates' of local teachers' colleges. Though I was not yet a diplomate, I was one of those participants, representing my school principal because I had shown an interest in working with children with learning difficulties and was producing successful results. My direction in life was sealed at that moment. I felt empowered and the synergy experienced during the sessions motivated me further and I returned to my school with renewed vigour. At these workshops I became involved with a group of bright young people and some seniors within the special education system in Trinidad and Tobago and we became known as The Association for Special Education of Trinidad and Tobago (TASETT). We agreed that while the CIDA programme was exciting and a good starting point for teachers in the system, the workshops focused upon awareness-raising rather than upon rigorous training and, as such, did not adequately prepare teachers for improving the quality of education in the classroom. As TASETT, we asked ourselves searching questions about what we wanted for special education, for our country, our teachers and our children. We decided that our teachers should have access to a high standard of tertiary education with certificated internationally recognized qualifications.

We researched several education systems and, together with senior educators from our education system, we developed what we perceived to be a desirable curriculum framework. We established a partnership with the national teachers' association, the Trinidad and Tobago Unified Teachers Association (T&TUTA), and together we set out to revolutionize special education in our country. Several universities were approached to support the venture and the University of Sheffield in the UK agreed to partner with us.

The *Marge Report* (1984) estimated there to be approximately 28,500 'handicapped' children in Trinidad and Tobago whose educational needs were not being met, although most were attending mainstream primary schools. It was acknowledged that collectively the 10 special schools only catered to less than 5 per cent of the children with special needs, and there were insufficient trained teachers at these schools to meet even the needs of the students who attended them. In light of this situation, the Marge Report suggested 'gradually adjusting the mainstream schools to meet the needs of those special children already in them' (Ministry of Education, 1985: 64). Though the government acknowledged the importance of the Marge Report by including the general findings and recommendations in the Education Plan (1985–1990), it still appeared hesitant to invest its funds in this area on non-economic return. While seemingly acknowledging their responsibility to provide 'Special Education at all levels of the Education System' the Plan preceded that acceptance of responsibility by stating that the country 'must proceed with caution and seek alternatives which are educationally and socially acceptable, but which are not demanding on the public purse' (Ministry of Education, 1985: 63).

Educators at all levels of the system began to realize that special education should be a concern of all people and that it involved the delivery of quality education to all students. Teachers and parents who once seemed voiceless had developed a voice and were able at that point to recognize and articulate that they needed more specialized training in special education. They were willing to be 'pioneering foot-soldiers' in a system which was at this point devoid of developed support arrangements for special education. They were therefore encouraged to become members of organizations like TASETT. I remember arguing strongly against the use of the term 'special' because I felt that the term should be replaced by quality. My argument was that people did not live in a regular world and a special world. The world was one place and we all had to live in it.

A Special Education Elective was only introduced at the Teachers' College in Trinidad and Tobago in 1988 and offered to a handful of students (maximum 10). I was one of those students. I challenged the old knowledge of labelling children based on the medical model and introduced my colleagues to the emerging thinking in different parts of the world on the social model of disability.

In Trinidad and Tobago, a new breed of teacher-educator was emerging. It was a time of much excitement and eager anticipation. So determined was TASETT to make a positive impact that they recruited the support of the best lecturers available on the islands – the Dean and other lecturers of the Faculty of Education, University of the West Indies and senior officers of the Ministry of Education. Senior advocates of special education and teachers who had special skills and experiences with working with children who had different disabilities were also invited to share their knowledge and experiences with the group of students. Lecturers from the University of Sheffield were also invited to conduct a vacation school twice a year and the university was approached to validate the course. We insisted that they work with us as a team and not tell us how to approach our problems 'correctly' from their perspective. We taught them post-colonial theory.

The decision of a group of local educators in 1987 to develop a certificate/ diploma course in Special Education for interested teachers in the country was based on struggles around the interpretation and enactment of educational policy and the quality of provision of teacher professional education in the country. This was a project which sought to reconceptualize the meanings of social justice, human rights and the delivery of adequate educational services to children with special educational needs in a post-colonial society. These children included those who for any reason experienced difficulty in learning and so did not fall into any special category of disability. We supported the provision of quality education for all.

Initially, the main impetus for change came from teachers working collectively through The Association for Special Education of Trinidad and Tobago and the Special Education Committee of T&TUTA to address the shortage of trained teachers in the area of special education. The process of this struggle contributed to sustaining the momentum and vitality of a shared vision. This vision was part of a self-liberating movement where teacher-participants were encouraged to become reflective practitioners in the process of self-empowerment. The relationship with the University of Sheffield developed as a result of an ongoing consultative-collaborative approach to teacher education which was 'firmly rooted in the on-going discourse between teachers and their organizations and the University' (Armstrong and Namsoo, 2000: 209).

The pioneering group (course participants as well as the management committee) recognized that long sought after change in education was not coming from the technocrats and the bureaucrats of the Ministry of Education but from the creativity and effort generated by the struggle for social justice and rights. Out of this grew the 'revolutionary' idea of changing schools and, by extension, the education system as a whole into something more inclusive and more appropriate to the conditions and aspirations of a developing country. With the new tools of education came liberation for some, and children who were probably 'faceless bunches' in the schools were now recognized and included in the processes of change and learning. These struggles are ongoing. There is no 'quick fix' solution but taking ownership of the agenda for inclusion within one's own school, community and country allows educators to contest the power relationships of schooling which so often construct the role of schools as mechanisms for selection and exclusion.

Along the way, I have gained considerable experience of working strategically with governments. I had been employed for approximately eight years at a senior level on two national World Bank projects. This provided me with an intimate understanding of international funding agencies and the somewhat crippling conditions attached to development projects. I felt fiercely protective of the five cohorts of 28,000 young people who had left the formal education system in my country since independence in 1963 without any marketable skills. I understood how cultural definitions of success could exclude young people who were struggling for a chance to succeed in their fragile vocations, from the labour market.

In 1998, I read for a PhD at the University of Sheffield. Though the research was located within the Caribbean, consideration was given to the effects of globalization and the role of international funding agencies on the education systems of developing states and how world classifications are constructed in a manner which tie these countries into states of dependency. The thesis also emphasized the importance of collaborations and alliances among funding agencies, governmental bodies and NGOs to enhance development initiatives. These collaborations need to be developed at all levels of the system, and in particular include practising teachers in action research and curriculum development.

In 2001, I was employed with the University of Sheffield, in the School of Education as Director of the Caribbean Distance Education Programme. I had come full circle from being a member of the team who designed the first programme to directing and expanding the entire programme. I was still struggling with the notion of inclusion. I could not understand why people were excluded in the first place. As a black person in a white country I was, for the first time, directly confronted with racism and exclusion. As a Trinidadian, a black person from a black country, I struggled with this experience and found it difficult to understand how some people thought that I was not like everyone else. Despite the challenges, I have continued on this journey, working in teacher education and professional development in England, in the Caribbean and now in Australia. In particular, I have come to understand that for inclusion to be meaningful it is not sufficient to put forward the idea of education for all. Inclusive education has to transform the experience and lives of those who study and work in education at all levels and to do so it has to challenge the discriminations of educational privilege (not of course excellence). And educational partnerships between developed and developing countries should have at their heart a willingness on the part of the privileged from the first world to learn from their developing world partners and question and transform their own systems as an outcome of that learning.

Today in Australia, I look at my career and reflect on how I now see the world. Inclusion is a tricky concept. I am still confused but I do believe in meaningful dialogue and respect for other people's positions in life and their opinions. I have moved from understanding inclusion purely as a special needs construct to understanding it in the broader sense of diversity involving all people of the world regardless of their race, ethnicity, gender, sexual orientation, differing disabilities, native language, native country of origin, and so on. I still hold on to the belief of the delivery of quality services to all and, in my current role at the University of Sydney, I ensure that my students are all treated with the utmost respect because they too have their stories and their learning journeys.

Derrick's journey

At the age of 11 I failed a test that would have considerable bearing on my future education and life. I hardly remember taking the test and when I discovered that I had failed it, I had no concerns because every single person in my primary school class failed the same test. The outcome was a non-academic secondary education pathway, a secondary modern school, in the old English tripartite system. It was obvious to anyone who looked that the quality of education that followed was poor, but that was hardly relevant to someone 'destined' for a working-class job in a working-class town in the north of England. I stayed on at school until I was 16, although I could have left at 15, but another year at school simply put off work in some dead-end job so it seemed like a good idea, and at the end of it I even passed an 'O' level examination – only one mind you.

After I left school, for some reason, and I still have no idea why, I became interested in learning. It was like waking up late from a dream. I was so far behind, so ignorant of everything and so excited to start catching up with my day while it was still light. In fact the days were long and I worked incredibly hard to pass the examinations that would eventually get me into university. But university was such a nightmare. The staff members were very nice, but had not met many people like me, and my fellow students, sometimes in good heart but often with patronizing malice, made fun of my working-class accent and my strange 'northern' behaviours. Naively I thought that a university education was about learning and about using knowledge for useful purposes. The reality for many members in those so old-fashioned university communities was that knowledge was a 'game'. The very point of it was that it had no relevance. For many of the lecturing staff it was merely a continuation of their school, a school of perpetual privilege and life-avoidance. For my fellow students it was a rite of passage into the comforts of middle-class privilege. I got my degree and left and did not look back for nearly 20 years.

My own life-avoidance was at an end, or perhaps I realized that there was not really any such thing – this was my life. I worked at many different jobs over the next few years, but mostly as a welder and later, when industrial collapse brought hard times to engineering, steel, shipbuilding and construction industries in the UK, I became a taxi driver. I trained at night school – three nights a week – to become a skilled craftsman welder, only to see it blown away as Britain de-industrialized and instead became a financial centre for the rich. Where to now?

It was back to college, part-time, to study to be a teacher in adult education. Two young children and scraping a living with a full-time night job as a taxi driver. I was lucky and privileged to meet and be mentored by a number of outstanding educators as I moved through teachers' college, a Master's degree in education, a PhD and back into academia working in the field of Education. People change your life. I should name them: Rob Newton, Les Smith, David Galloway, Sally Tomlinson, Len Barton and Wilfred Carr.

The idea of inclusion is so complex it is difficult to know whether it really means anything at all. As a child I was happy but I did not know that decisions were being taken about me that excluded me and that would lead to my exclusion from so many opportunities, including the opportunity to be educated. I did not feel excluded. All my friends went to the same school. We enjoyed school, though not because of the learning that took place but more so because of growing up among friends. In that sense, clearly school was exceptionally inclusive! When I finally did get the opportunity to go to university, one consequence was that I lost contact with all my friends back home. We no longer had the same things in common and, as much as the angst over my identity increased during these years, I was certainly no longer part of my childhood community of friends. So educational access brought social isolation. And then because I wasn't a part of the university community I returned to my own roots and re-created my own world, but this time as an adult, and yet, it was a very different world.

The lesson that I have drawn from my own life has been that educational opportunity is framed by one's personal history and one's social and cultural background. It is not determined by these circumstances but it is framed in the sense that a person has no choice but to make active choices. Yet, these choices are not simplistic ones about taking or not taking opportunities for self-improvement. The nature of inclusion or exclusion in respect of any community is defined by those communities in the context of their structural relation to the broader society in which the relations of power between different groups are played out. Some are more permeable than others but even the most vulnerable of groups can establish formal or informal rules that indicate who will be accepted, and often do erect barriers of social exclusion, yet the reason for the group itself being disadvantaged and denied genuine access to opportunities is rarely of its own making.

In my research and teaching in the field of inclusive education I have worked on issues of the assessment processes by which young people come to be identified as having 'emotional and behavioural difficulties' and, as a consequence, receive different types of educational intervention. I have worked with adults who when children were labelled as having 'learning difficulties' and placed in special schools or classes, and in some cases into long-term institutional settings. One of the most exciting experiences in my research career was working with disabled people with 'learning difficulties' in the self-advocacy movement. Observing the ways in which people labelled, marginalized and discriminated against use their collective endeavours to confront and challenge a disabling society was inspiring. Yet alongside this were examples of 'self-advocacy' groups established by institutions for their inmates and run by the institution itself as a social activity. I have also worked with young people who for one reason or another find themselves in contact with the criminal justice system. Here again the nature of inclusion and exclusion is defined and enforced by peer groups, families and local communities as well as by the institutions of the state – schools, the courts, the welfare services and the youth offender institutions. Young people navigate these different processes of inclusion and exclusion, often successfully, sometimes not so – but then who 'defines' success?

I have also worked in international education, spending nine years in collaborations with teachers, teachers' organizations and Ministries of Education in the countries of the Caribbean. When one begins to work in the developing world it is easy to imagine that one is bringing enlightenment and new learning to a group of people who are eager to learn – and in my experience teachers in the developing world are certainly eager to learn. It is worth taking a few minutes to step back from this comment to appreciate the racism that lies deeply embedded in such beliefs. A missionary approach to education in the developing world disregards and devalues the very real struggles that people have engaged in to develop their education systems. Education in many countries has been a major

vehicle for social change and part of the traditions of anti-colonial struggles across the world. To question people's knowledge of the power of education in these contexts is not only patronizing but deeply demeaning. It
also de-politicizes the issue of education, representing educational development as a technical enterprise of improvement and efficiency gains. In
developing countries, inclusive education is not about the management of
troublesome children or the optimization of cost efficiencies. It actually is
about inclusion. And it is not simply about inclusion within a country, but
is concerned with the much broader issue of international inclusion – the
ongoing struggle for recognition and place in the world. The relationship
between power and education is much better understood in the developing world in my experience than it is in the developed world, and that is
because of the unevenness of power across these two worlds. In the developing world, the history of education carries with it the history of colonial
oppression (the denial of access to education in slave times for instance)
and the contribution of educational thought to political liberation in the
anti-colonial movements.

There is no justification for working in the education field across two countries unless there is a genuine partnership between those involved in the
work. That is precisely where so much of the funded interventions by international development agencies break down because they are founded on
the premise that there is good practice in the developed world that needs to
be imported into the developing world. That sort of policy transfer is meaningless. Sometimes, educators in developing countries may see some aspect
of policy or practice in another country that they choose to develop or
apply within their own systems. That is a fairly normal part of cross-
border learning. But where educators from two countries work together, the
critical issue has to be the mutual learning and development that takes
place. Ideally, it should involve a partnership that is also multi-focused on
education in both countries. Certainly there has to be willingness on the
part of those who work outside their own context to learn from the engagement, and to use that learning to critique their own experience and to
employ that critique as part of an educational development activity within
their own situation. That is the nature of mutuality and partnership.
Developing countries face many issues in building national educational systems that meet national and individual needs and aspirations in today's
world. They face these challenges in the context of local as well as international politics which may optimize or undermine the aspirations that many
educators have. Nonetheless, there is also much to be learned from working
with these challenges about the relations of power within and between
countries. Yet it is the mutuality of critical engagement that distinguishes
any educational intervention, strategy, policy or practice as inclusive. In

other words, the real essence of inclusive education lies in a respect for mutual learning.

Ilektra's journey

The space that 'inclusion' in education occupies as an academic field is a peculiar one. As many people in the field, I come from a background that blurs the boundaries between general and special education. A short historical account will briefly sketch my own engagement with inclusion. My early encounters with issues surrounding inclusion and the political dimension of the education of disabled students (Zoniou-Sideri, 1996) as part of my undergraduate studies in Greece developed and determined my current position in the field of inclusive education.

After graduating, I worked as a 'support' teacher in a pilot project, including a disabled student in a regular school; the year was 1994, the same year that UNESCO's Salamanca Statement was produced. In that project, I saw first hand what was possible; I worked collaboratively with the classroom teacher who was also an excellent mentor for a new teacher like myself, the curriculum was planned collaboratively with input from the parents, the available support was used for the student for whom the project was designed for but also for the rest of the classroom and so on. The project was successful but at the same time, I was concerned about whether what we were doing was making a difference beyond the classroom since attitudes of disability as a personal tragedy from parents and other school staff were expressed despite the success of inclusion. I was also worried that in trying to change these attitudes we emphasized achievements that reinforced existing understandings of normality.

Soon after, I embarked on a Master's degree in Special and Inclusive Education at the University of Sheffield in England. One of the reasons that I wanted to study further was to explore how as a teacher I could become better in implementing inclusion. The teaching staff working in that programme included Len Barton, Felicity Armstrong, Peter Clough and one of the co-authors of this book, Derrick Armstrong. We engaged with the social model of disability, inclusion as political struggle and critical theory. I did not find 'easy' answers on how to 'do' inclusion, but rather a language to develop my understanding of inclusion and to inform my practice. I undertook my PhD at the same department and started engaging in academic activities; researching, presenting in conferences, writing and so on. My areas of interests were inclusion as it is defined in policy and it is contested in its implementation in different educational systems.

Almost 10 years after graduating from the University of Athens, I returned to Greece working mainly as a researcher but also tutoring in in-service and post-graduate courses. I was back into teaching but this time I was teaching about inclusion and special education. Increasingly in these seven years, the last three in Australia, teaching has become my central activity. I am teaching in what can be described as the 'hybrid' field of 'special and inclusive education'.

I teach in *general* teacher education programmes as well as *special* teacher education programmes. Some of the students in these programmes already work or will work in special schools or special units in regular schools. I have taught and researched with colleagues who identify themselves with inclusive, special education or both. In the faculties that I have worked there are other colleagues who teach research on other aspects of diversity or specialist educational topics. I have engaged in research with pre-service teachers, teachers, principals, parents, and students and adults with and without disabilities.

In all these activities *what* inclusion is and *if* and *how* it can be realized is central. In many instances I find myself reflecting on the contradictions, dilemmas, and restrictions that I face in similar ways that teachers and schools reflect on theirs; what I am doing is governed by the ways that the departments and programmes are structured in which special – and/or inclusive education – is defined as a specialist field of education referring to specific groups of children and young people; the accreditation requirements that our students need to demonstrate at graduation – with different requirements for the distinct groups of general and special teachers; the limited time that we have to translate these requirements into learning outcomes and engage with them in the classroom; the expectations of our students when enrolling in our courses – looking for ways that will clearly work in their classrooms; the characteristics of the systems where our students will work as teachers – systems with specific continua of settings and support provision, classification systems that are used for identification, administration and educational purposes, and curricula outcomes and performance expectations; and, of course, the other expectations of my work in terms of research, administration and performance indicators.

Booth (2003: 51) refers to a paradigmatic war between 'special needs education', on the one hand, and 'equality and diversity' approaches to inclusion, on the other, in teacher education institutions, schools and policy which in part constitutes a 'clash between assimilationist and transformative perspectives on inclusion'. Slee (2006: 113) describes how what I call the 'hybrid field of special and inclusive education' has been developed and asks whether the reformist agenda for inclusive education has been 'irrevocably undermined or sent up an epistemological cul de sac by a thoughtless dalliance with special educational needs'.

How do I locate my own practice in this paradigmatic clash? The answer is simple; with great uneasiness. I strongly believe that it is through inclusion as a transformative project that the ability/disability and normality/diversity dichotomies can be essentially challenged. However, this transformative project has yet to develop an alternative to the existing educational arrangements which are based on and reinforce ability/disability and normality/diversity dichotomies. Engaging in educational practice within existing educational arrangements requires a set of tools that can allow navigating them (what works), which can be called a pragmatic approach to inclusion, but at the same time a critical under-standing of the limitations of both the successes and failures of our efforts.

In an interview published in *Educational Philosophy and Theory*, the interviewers asked Iris Marion Young in which of the five faces of oppression she has iden-tified she will place education (Sardoč and Shaughnessy, 2001: 95). Young responded that 'I don't see that education is a concept of oppression. The five faces that I identify are all concepts referring to forms of wrongs that can be done to people. Education is not in itself a wrong that is done to people, at least I hope not.' She continues that the educational system in the USA – and it can be argued in any country – reproduces oppressions but at the same time 'there are many educators and counter-hegemonic educational materials and loca-tions that aim to undo those effects' (ibid.: 95–6). This critical understanding and reflection on our own practice, of those that we work with and of the con-text that we are operating in can be rendered into self-indulgence or it can immobilize us without a transformative project for inclusion that is realizable.

In an ethnographic study of inclusion in England and Greece, I argued that none of the participants, students, teachers, teachers' assistants, perceived education and school as 'totally' inclusive or exclusive but rather as 'condi-tionally' inclusive or exclusive (Spandagou, 2002). It is this 'conditionality' of 'reality' in perceiving inclusion/exclusion at present and in the future that is described in Marcuse's (1968: 154) statement that 'the freedom of imagina-tion disappears to the extent that real freedom becomes a real possibility'.

 A final reflection and activity

Readers of this book may also experience multiple roles that force them to reflect on where they are located in the inclusive education field and how they can resolve the dilemmas and tensions they face.

One constructive way to face these dilemmas and tensions and seek a way forward is through an exploration of one's own understanding of the meaning of inclusive education in the context of one's own life experiences.

(Continued)

(Continued)

- Write a brief life story of your own experience of inclusion and exclusion.
- What personal lessons have you drawn from these experiences and how have they informed your approach to the idea and practice of inclusive education?
- Find a colleague or colleagues you feel comfortable sharing stories with. Are there ways in which your understanding of inclusion has changed as a result of this sharing?
- How would you and your colleagues collectively address what you each identify as key issues in implementing a policy or programme of inclusive education?

References

Abberley, P. (1996) 'Work, utopia and impairment', in L. Barton (ed.), *Disability and Society: Emerging Issues and Insights*. London: Longman.

Abbott, W.K. and Snidal, D. (2000) 'Hard and soft law in international governance', *International Organization*, 54(3): 421–56.

Ainscow, M., Booth, T. and Dyson, A., with Farrell, P., Frankham, J., Gallannaugh, F., Howes, A. and Smith, R. (2006) *Improving Schools, Developing Inclusion*. London: Routledge.

Alexander, R. (2003) 'For Blair 1997 is year zero', *Times Educational Supplement* (Friday Magazine), 19 September, p. 11.

Allan, J. (2008) *Rethinking Inclusive Education: The Philosophers of Difference in Practice*. Dordrecht: Springer.

Appadurai, A. (1993) 'Disjuncture and difference in the global cultural economy', In P. Williams and L. Chrisman (eds), *Colonial Discourse and Post-Colonial Theory: A Reader*. Hemel Hempstead: Harvester Wheatsheaf.

Armstrong, D. (1995) *Power and Partnership in Education; Parents, Children and Special Educational Needs*. London: Routledge.

Armstrong, D. (2005) 'Reinventing "Inclusion": New Labour and the cultural politics of special education', *Oxford Review of Education*, 31(1): 135–51.

Armstrong, D. and Namsoo[1], A.C. (2000) 'New Markets or New Alliances? Distance Education, Globalisation and Post Colonial Challenges.' *Distance Education in Small States: Conference Proceedings, Jamaica (WI) 27–28 July, 2000*. Jamaica, University of the West Indies Distance Education Centre (UWIDEC). pp. 207–212.

Australian Commonwealth (2005) *Disability Standards for Education (2005)*. Canberra: Australian Commonwealth.

Australian Commonwealth (1992) *Disability Discrimination Act*. Canberra: Australian Commonwealth.

Barnes, C. and Mercer, G. (2004) *Disability*. Cambridge: Polity Press.

Barton, L. (1995) 'The politics of education for all', *Support for Learning*, 10(4): 156–60.

Barton, L. (1997) 'Inclusive education: romantic, subversive or realistic?', *International Journal of Inclusive Education*, 1(3): 231–40.

Bateman, B. (1995) 'Who, how, and where: special education's issues in perpetuity', in J. Kauffman and D. Hallahan (eds), *The Illusion of Full Inclusion: A Comprehensive Critique of a Current Special Education Bandwagon*. Austin, TX: ProEd.

Bauman, Z. (1990) *Thinking Sociologically*, Oxford: Blackwell.

Beecher, G. (2005) 'Disability Standards: the challenge of achieving compliance with the Disability Discrimination Act', *Australian Journal of Human Rights*, 13(2): 139–70.

Berliner, D. and Biddle, B. (1995) *The Manufactured Crisis: Myths, Fraud, and the Attack on America's Public Schools*. New York: Longman.

---

[1] Publications prior to 2002 are in the name of Namsoo. Ann Cheryl's surname is now Armstrong.

Bhabha, H. (1994) *The Location of Culture.* London: Routledge.

Black-Hawkins, K., Florian, L. and Rouse, M. (2007) *Achievement and Inclusion in Schools.* London: Routledge.

Bloomberg News (2000) 'World Bank to Stop Pushing Poor to Pay for Health Care, School', Bloomberg News, 25 October.

Booth, T. (1995) 'Mapping inclusion and exclusion: concepts for all?', in C. Clark, A. Dyson and A. Millard (eds), *Towards Inclusive Schools?* London: David Fulton.

Booth, T. (2003) 'Views from the institution: overcoming barriers to inclusive teacher education?', in T. Booth, K. Nes and M. Strømstad (eds), *Developing Inclusive Teacher Education.* London: Routledge Falmer.

Booth, T. and Ainscow, M. (2002) *Index for Inclusion. Developing Learning and Participation in Schools.* Bristol: CSIE Ltd.

Brine, J. (1999) *Undereducating Women: Globalizing Inequality.* Buckingham: Open University Press.

Carr, W. and Hartnett, A. (1996) *Education and the Struggle for Democracy: The Politics of Educational Ideas.* Buckingham: Open University Press.

Carr-Hill, R. (2004) Book review on 'Education for all; is the world on track? EFA Global Monitoring Report 2002, Paris: UNESCO', *International Journal of Educational Development,* 24: 330–2.

Chossudovsky, M. (1994) 'Global impoverishment and the IMF-World Bank economic medicine', *MNC Masala.* Available from: www.corpwatch.org/feature/india/globalization/imfwb.html and http://aidc.org.za/archives/global_imp_and_IMF.html (accessed 5 November 2000).

Clements, L. and Read, J. (2008) 'Introduction: life, disability and the pursuit of human rights', in L. Clements and J. Read (eds), *Disabled People and the Right to Life: The Protection and Violation of Disabled People's Most Basic Human Rights.* London: Routledge.

Connell, R. (2007) *Southern Theory: The Global Dynamics of Knowledge in Social Science.* Sydney: Allen & Unwin.

Corbett, J. (2001) *Supporting Inclusive Education: A Connective Pedagogy.* London: Taylor & Francis.

Department for Children, Schools and Families (DCSF) (2008) *Education and Training Statistics for the United Kingdom* (additional information – schools). Available from: www.dcsf.gov.uk/trends/upload/xls/3_5t.xls

Department for Education (DfE) (1994) *Code of Practice on the Identification and Assessment of Special Educational Needs.* London: DfE.

Department for Education and Employment (DfEE) (1997a) *Excellence in Education.* London: DfEE.

Department for Education and Employment (DfEE) (1997b) *Excellence for All Children: Meeting Special Educational Needs.* London: DfEE.

Department for Education and Skills (DfES) (2001) *Special Educational Needs: Code of Practice.* London: DfES.

Department for Education and Skills (DfES) (2003) *Every Child Matters.* London: The Stationery Office.

Department for Education and Skills (DfES) (2004) *Removing Barriers to Achievement: The Government's Strategy for SEN.* London: DfES Publications.

Department of Education and Science (DES) (1978) *Special Educational Needs: Report of the Committee of Enquiry into the Education of Handicapped Children and Young People.* The Warnock Report. London: HMSO.

Dessent, T. (1987) *Making the Ordinary School Special.* Lewes: Falmer Press.

Dyson, A. (1999) 'Inclusion and inclusions: theories and discourses in inclusive education', in H. Daniels and P. Garner (eds), *Inclusive Education: Supporting Inclusion in Education Systems*. London: Kogan Page.

Education, Audiovisual and Culture Executive Agency (EACEA) (2009) *Early Childhood Education and Care in Europe: Tackling Social and Cultural Inequalities*. Brussels: EACEA and Eurydice.

European Agency for Development in Special Needs Education (EADSNE) (2003) *Special Needs Education in Europe: Thematic Publication*. Brussels: EADSNE.

European Commission (EC) (2000) *Key Data on Education in Europe 1999–2000*. Luxembourg: European Commission.

European Commission (EC) (2002) *Key Data on Education in Europe 2002*. Luxembourg: European Commission.

European Commission (EC) (2005) *Key Data on Education in Europe 2005*. Luxembourg: European Commission.

European Parliament (2009) *Fact Sheets on the European Union*. Strasburg: European Parliament. Available from: www.europarl.europa.eu/ (accessed 6 April 2009).

Eurydice (2004) *Integrating Immigrant Children into Schools in Europe*. Brussels: Eurydice.

Eurydice (2006) *Specific Educational Measures to Promote all Forms of Giftedness at School in Europe*. Brussels: Eurydice.

Florian, L., Hollenweger, J., Simeonsoon, R., Wedell, K., Riddell, S., Terzi, L. and Holland, A. (2006) 'Cross-cultural perspectives on the classification of children with disabilities; Part 1. Issues in the classification of children with disabilities', *Journal of Special Education*, 40(1): 36–45.

Foucault, M. (1967) *Madness and Civilization: A History of Insanity in the Age of Reason*. London: Tavistock.

Fulcher, G. (1989) *Disabling Policies? A Comparative Approach to Educational Policy and Disability*. London: Falmer Press.

Gamble, A. (1988) *The Free Economy and the Strong State*. London: Macmillan.

Giangreco, M. (1997) 'Key lessons learned about inclusive education: summary of the 1996 Schonnell Memorial Lecture', *International Journal of Disability, Development and Education*, 44(3): 193–206.

Giddens, A. (1990) *The Consequences of Modernity*. Cambridge: Polity Press.

Graham, L. and Slee, R. (2008) 'An illusory interiority: interrogating the discourse/s of inclusion', *Educational Philosophy and Theory*, 40(2): 277–93.

Harvey-Koelpin, S. (2006) 'The impact of reform on students with disabilities', in E. Brantlinger (ed.), *Who Benefits from Special Education? Remediating (Fixing) Other People's Children*, Mahwah, NJ: Lawrence Erlabaum Associates.

Heung, V. and Grossman, D. (2007) 'Inclusive education as a strategy for achieving education for all: perspectives from three Asian societies', in D.P. Baker and A.W. Wiseman (eds), *Education for All: Global Promises, National Challenges*. International Perspectives on Education and Society, vol. 8.

HMSO (2001) *Special Educational Needs and Disability Act*. London: HMSO.

Hoogvelt, A. (1997) *Globalisation and the Postcolonial World: A New Political Economy of Development*. London: Macmillan.

Itkonen, T. and Jahnukainen, M. (2007) 'An analysis of accountability policies in Finland and the United States', *International Journal of Disability, Development and Education*, 54(1): 5–23.

Jones, P. (1992) *World Bank Financing of Education: Lending, Learning and Development*. London: Routledge.

Jones, P.W. and Coleman, D. (2005) *The United Nations and Education: Multilateralism, Development and Globalization*. New York: Routledge Falmer.

Kapur, D., Lewis, J. and Webb, R. (eds) (1997) *The World Bank: Its First Half Century. History*. Washington, DC: Brookings Institution Press.

Law 3699/2008 [Greek] (2008) *Special Education Law for Ensuring Equal Opportunities for People with a Disability and Special Educational Needs*. Athens: Government Gazette.

Lawson, J. and Silver, H. (1973) *A Social History of Education in England*. London: Methuen.

Leo, E. and Barton, L. (2006) 'Inclusion, diversity and leadership: perspectives, possibilities and contradictions', *Educational Management, Administration and Leadership*, 34(2): 167–80.

Lipsky, D.K. and Gartner, A. (1997) *Inclusion and School Reform: Transforming America's Classrooms*, Baltimore, MD: Paul H. Brookes.

Lister, R. (1997) *Citizenship: Feminist Perspectives*. London: Macmillan Press.

Mabbett, D. (2005) 'The development of rights-based social policy in the European Union: the example of disability rights. *Journal of Common Market Studies*, 43(1): 97–120.

Marcuse, H. (1968) *Negations; Essays in Critical Theory*, London: Allen Lane, Penguin Press [with translations from the German by J. Shapiro].

Marge, M. (1984) *Report on the Survey of the Incidence of Handicapping Conditions in Children between the Ages of 3 and 16 in Trinidad & Tobago*. Commissioned by the Ministry of Education, Republic of Trinidad and Tobago, sponsored by the Organisation of American States.

Mayo, P. (1999) *Gramsci, Freire and Adult Education: Possibilities for Transformative Action*. New York: Zed Books.

McCulloch, G. (1994) *Educational Reconstruction: The 1944 Education Act and the Twenty-First Century*, Ilford, Essex: Woburn Press.

McMichael, P. (1995) 'The new colonialism: global regulation and the restructuring of the inter-state system', *Contributions in Economics and Economic History*, 1(164): 37–55.

Ministry of Education, Government of Trinidad and Tobago (1985) *Education Plan 1985–1990*. Republic of Trinidad and Tobago.

Minow, M. (1985) 'Learning to live with the dilemma of difference: bilingual and special education', *Law and Contemporary Problems*, 48(2): 157–211.

Mundy, K. (2007) 'Education for All: paradoxes and prospects of a global promise', in D.P. Baker and A.W. Wiseman (eds), *Education for All: Global Promises, National Challenges*, International Perspectives on Education and Society, vol. 8.

National Commission on Excellence in Education (1983) *A Nation at Risk: The Imperative for Educational Reform*. Washington: U.S. Department of Education.

Norwich, B. (2008) *Dilemmas of Difference, Inclusion and Disability*. London: Routledge.

Nussbaum, M. (2006) *Frontiers of Justice: Disability, Nationality, Species Membership*. Belknap Press of Harvard University Press: Cambridge, MA.

OECD (2003) *Education Policy Analysis*. Paris: CERI-OECD.

Office for Standards in Education (Ofsted) (2000) *Evaluating Educational Inclusion: Guidance for Inspectors and Schools*, e-document available from www.ofsted.gov.uk

Oliver, M. (1996) *Understanding Disability: From Theory to Practice*. London: Macmillan Press.

Priestley, M. (2007) 'In search of European disability policy: between national and global', *European Journal of Disability Research*, 1(1): 61–74.

Pritchard, D.G. (1963) *Education and the Handicapped 1760–1960.* London: Routledge and Kegan Paul.

Rawls, J. (1999) *A Theory of Justice.* Revised edition. Oxford: Oxford University Press.

Rose, N. (1999) *Governing the Soul: The Shaping of the Private Self.* 2nd edition. London: Free Association Books.

Rutter, M., Maughn, B., Mortimore, P., Ouston, J. and Smith, A. (1979) *Fifteen Thousand Hours: Secondary Schools and Their Effects on Pupils.* London: Open Books.

Sardoč, M. and Shaughnessy, M.F. (2001) 'An interview with Iris Marion Young', *Educational Philosophy and Theory*, 33(1): 95–101.

Sen, A. (2003) The Importance of Basic Education in *EducationGuardian.co.uk*, 28 October. Available from: http://people.cis.ksu.edu/~ab/Miscellany/basiced.html (accessed 18 March 2009).

Shakespeare, T. (2006) *Disability Rights and Wrongs.* London: Routledge.

Silvers, A. and Francis, L. (2005) 'Justice through trust: disability and the "Outlier Problem" in social contract theory', *Ethics*, 116: 40–76.

Sindelar, P.T., Shearer, D.K., Yendol-Hoppey, D. and Liebert T.W. (2006) 'The Sustainability of inclusive school reform', *Exceptional Children*, 72(3): 317–31.

Slee, R. (1996) 'Clauses of conditionality: the "reasonable" accommodation of language', in L. Barton (ed.), *Disability and Society: Emerging Issues and Insights.* London: Longman.

Slee, R. (2006) 'Limits to and possibilities for educational reform', *International Journal of Inclusive Education*, 10(2–3): 109–19.

Smith, A. (1998) 'Crossing borders: learning from inclusion and restructuring research in Sweden, Denmark, Norway, and the United States', *International Journal of Educational Research*, 29: 161–6.

Smith, T. and Motivans, A. (2007) 'Teacher quality and education for all in sub-Saharan Africa', in D.P. Baker and A.W. Wiseman (eds), *Education for All: Global Promises, National Challenges.* International Perspectives on Education and Society, vol. 8.

Spandagou, I. (2002) 'Comparative and ethnographic research on inclusion: the case of English and Greek secondary education', unpublished PhD thesis, University of Sheffield.

Tawney, R.H. (1952) *Equality.* 4th edition. London: George Allen and Unwin.

Terzi, L. (2005) 'Beyond the dilemma of difference. The capability approach to disability and special educational needs', *Journal of Philosophy of Education*, 39(3): 443–59.

The United Nations and Human Rights (1948) *Universal Declaration of Human Rights*, G.A. res. 217A (III), U.N. Doc A/810 at 71 (1948) Department of Public Information. New York: United Nations.

Thomas, G. and Loxley, A. (2001) *Deconstructing Special Education and Constructing Inclusion.* Buckingham: Open University Press.

Thomas, G., Walker, D. and Webb, J. (1998) *The Making of the Inclusive School*, London: Routledge.

Tomlinson, S. (1981) *Educational Subnormality: A Study in Decision-making.* London: Routledge, Kegan and Paul.

Tomlinson, S. (1982) *A Sociology of Special Education.* London: Routledge.

UNESCO (1990) *'Background document: World Conference on Education for All – meeting basic learning needs'.* Available from http://unesdoc.unesco.org/images/0009/000975/097552e.pdf (accessed 30 October 2008).

UNESCO (1994) *The Salamanca Statement and Framework for Action on Special Needs Education*. Available from www.unesco.org/education/pdf/SALAMA_E.PDF (accessed 30 October 2008).

UNESCO (1996) *Education for all: Achieving the Goal-Final Report*, Mid-Decade Meeting of the International Consultative Forum on Education for All. Amman: UNESCO.

UNESCO (1996a) *Mid-Decade Review of Progress towards Education for All*. Paris: UNESCO.

UNESCO (1996b) *Education for all: Achieving the Goal – Final Report*, Mid-decade Meeting of the International Consultative Forum on Education for All. Amman: UNESCO.

UNESCO (2000) *Education for All: Meeting our Collective Commitments: Notes on the Dakar Framework for Action*. Paris: UNESCO.

UNESCO (2000) *The Americas–Education for All in the Americas: Regional Framework of Action*. Available online at: http://www2.unesco.org/wef/enleadup/regmeet_frame_ameri.shtm

UNESCO (2001) *Education for All – Background Documents: Information Kit on Education for All*. Available from www.unesco.org/education/efa/ed_for_all/background/background_kit_achieve_goal.shtml (accessed 15 February 2002).

UNESCO (2002a) *Universal Declaration on Cultural Diversity*. Paris: UNESCO.

UNESCO (2002b) EFA Global Monitoring Report 2002. *Education for All: Is the World on Track?* Paris: UNESCO.

UNESCO (2005) *Guidelines for Inclusion: Ensuring Access to Education for All*. Paris: UNESCO.

UNESCO (2006) *EFA Global Monitoring Report 2007. Strong Foundations: Early Childhood Care and Education*. Paris: UNESCO. Available from www.unesco.org/en/efareport/reports/2007-early-childhood/ (accessed on 20 April 2009).

UNESCO (2007) *EFA Global Monitoring Report 2008. Education for All by 2015: Will We Make It?* Paris: UNESCO. Available from www.unesco.org/en/efareport/reports/2008-mid-term-review/ (accessed on 16 March 2009).

UNESCO, Paris (France) and Ministry of Education and Science, Madrid (Spain) (1994) *World Conference on Special Needs Education: Access and Quality* (Salamanca, Spain, June 7–10, 1994) Final Report.

UN Non-Governmental Liaison Service (NGLS) with Gretchen Luchsinger (2008) *International Development Cooperation Today: Emerging Trends and Debates*. New York and Geneva: The United Nations Non-Governmental Liaison Service (NGLS).

United Nations (1993) *UN Standard Rules on the Equalization of Opportunities for Persons with Disabilities*. New York: United Nations.

United Nations (2006) *Convention on the Rights of Persons with Disabilities and Optional Protocol*. New York: United Nations.

United Nations (2008) *The Millennium Development Goals Report 2008*. New York: United Nations.

Velaskar, P. (1998) 'Ideology, education and the political struggle for liberation: change and challenge among the Dalits of Maharashtra', in S. Shukla and R. Kaul (eds), *Education, Development and Underdevelopment*. New Delhi: Sage Publications.

Vislie, L. (2003) 'From integration to inclusion; focusing global trends and changes in the western European societies', *European Journal of Special Needs Education*, 18(1): 17–35.

Vislie, L. (2006) 'Special education under the modernity. From restricted liberty, through organized modernity, to extended liberty and a plurality of practices', *European Journal of Special Needs Education*, 21(4): 395–414.

Warnock, M. (2005) *Special Educational Needs: A New Look* (Impact No 11). London: Philosophy of Education Society of Great Britain.

Wedell, K. (2005) 'Dilemmas in the quest for inclusion', *British Journal of Special Education*, 32(1): 3–11.

Williams, S. (2001) *The State of Early Childhood Provision in Dominica*. Available from www.uwichill. edu.bb/bnccde/dominica/conference/papers/Williams.html (accessed 20 March 2001).

Zoniou-Sideri, A. (1996) *Disabled People and Their Education; A Psycho-Pedagogic Approach to Inclusion*. 2nd edition. Athens: Greek Letters [in Greek].

Zoniou-Sideri, A., Deropoulou-Derou, E., Karagianni, P. and Spandagou, I. (2006) 'Inclusive discourse in Greece: strong voices, weak policies', *International Journal of Inclusive Education*, 10(2–3): 279–91.

Index